Yes! on Demand

YES! ON DEMAND

How to Create Winning, Customized Library Service

Kathy L. Middleton

Foreword by Rivkah Sass

LIBRARIES
UNLIMITED™
An Imprint of ABC-CLIO, LLC
Santa Barbara, California • Denver, Colorado

Copyright © 2017 by Kathy L. Middleton

All rights reserved. No part of this publication may be reproduced, stored in a retrieval system, or transmitted, in any form or by any means, electronic, mechanical, photocopying, recording, or otherwise, except for the inclusion of brief quotations in a review, without prior permission in writing from the publisher.

Yes! on Demand: How to Create Winning, Customized Library Service
Library of Congress Cataloging in Publication Control Number: 2016027467

ISBN: 978-1-4408-4853-7
EISBN: 978-1-4408-4854-4

21 20 19 18 17   1 2 3 4 5

This book is also available as an eBook.

Libraries Unlimited
An Imprint of ABC-CLIO, LLC

ABC-CLIO, LLC
130 Cremona Drive, P.O. Box 1911
Santa Barbara, California 93116-1911
www.abc-clio.com

This book is printed on acid-free paper ∞

Manufactured in the United States of America

Dedicated to Library Stars Everywhere

Contents

Foreword

Sometimes I worry that in our quest to find the next new library thing, we are so busy debating whatever our current library buzzwords are—future, relevancy, outcomes, library service—and so busy competing with one another to be the first to offer the latest new "thing" in library service, whatever that might be, that we forget the fundamentals of why we exist and what our customers need.

What makes a great library? The willingness to say "yes." There is nothing more exhilarating than encountering a customer at an outreach event and having that customer say, "We're unabashed library fans." It's validation that what we do matters, makes life better, and builds advocates. So how do we get there? By having the courage to address the elephant in the room: that sometimes we get in the way of ourselves, that we forget that frontline staff must be empowered to use their own good judgment in favor of the customer. That it's okay to have fun with customers and colleagues, and that libraries need to foster cultures that allow mistakes to happen, and finally that the best culture is a no-guilt culture.

This book addresses these issues and outlines why "yes" customer service is so critical to our success and to building passionate fans. We are always our best selves when we feel supported and valued in our roles, no matter what our roles might be. Let's get to "Yes!"

Rivkah Sass

Introduction

With a title like *Yes! on Demand*, you are probably wondering why I chose to begin this book with a list of no-nos. But I feel it is only fair that I first describe what this book is *not*. It is not a rigid set of rules for achieving the ideal state of customer service; it is not a compilation of charts, surveys, or statistics; and it is not an instruction manual on reporting tools or data gathering. The equation for the perfected library would be much easier to solve if all of our customers were exactly alike. They are not. In order to arrive at yes-focused results, each customer service transaction must be individualized for each customer's need. We sometimes rely much too heavily on research and studies before embarking on change, sometimes to the point of paralysis. How many opportunities have we lost to extended research and analysis? Let's push past the inclination to over-research and overanalyze in favor of delivering service based on what's already working in the most successful organizations in the world. In the spirit of providing great customer service, let's get started!

Librarians love to define words. The term "customer," which is used throughout this book, wins over other terms we regularly use: patron, visitor, user, client, guest, and borrower. "Customer" describes those who purchase (and borrow) products and services. For the sake of consistency and clarity in this work, I'll use the term "customer." Library customers transact business at service desks; they receive receipts, pay for lost cards or books, and also pay taxes for library service. There is a cost associated with operating a public library. The word "customer" shows respect for the person transacting business with the library and places him or her in the driver's seat. Customers have choices, and libraries must compete with others for their business. For a list and discussion of library customer terms, see Joseph Matthews's *The Customer-Focused Library*, which provides commonly used terms and descriptions for borrowers, card holders, registered borrowers, readers, clients, members, guests, and customers.[1]

Yes! on Demand customer service recognizes the challenges that many staff face working in public libraries today and promotes happiness and support for ourselves, our coworkers, and our customers. Winning retail businesses today embrace a simple and incredibly open and forgiving philosophy: allow employees the freedom to think independently and creatively to find solutions in the customer's favor. When the customer is happy, staff are happier, and the business (library) thrives due to customer loyalty and repeat business.

No-centric customer service drives library customers to other sources for information. They will pay for resources that are easier to access and are delivered in a yes-focused environment. Amazon or Barnes & Noble, for example, offer customized, no-hassle service. Yes-focused customer service brings new job satisfaction, happiness, and enjoyment, and above all, exceeds customer expectations. Many libraries are experiencing a decline in circulation or general library use. It seems silly to imagine a place that is devoted to delivering information and freedom of information worrying about keeping or gaining customers. But this is where we find ourselves today. Libraries provide the most comprehensive collection of materials at absolutely no cost, from many of the most educated and info-savvy people in the world, yet many people still perceive libraries as old fashioned and irrelevant.

How often have you been challenged to respond to the question of library relevance when someone realizes you're a public librarian? We hear, "I didn't know people still used libraries," and "Are you seeing a decline in library use?" or "Libraries are so quiet; it must be so nice to read all day." These are most likely customers who have moved on to find resources elsewhere—where they're easier to access and delivered by businesses primed to deliver personal service. For the customer looking for easy transactions, the library often presents a slow-moving institution bound by rules.

We can walk into any fast-food restaurant or retail business, or access any Web site, and immediately sense where to go and what we need to do to attend to our business. This is not always the case in libraries. Customers may find library layouts confusing. Library restrictions are magnified when the person behind the information desk does not look up to acknowledge customers or is too focused on a process or the computer screen. There are rules found in libraries that do not exist anywhere else—except maybe the Department of Motor Vehicles. Let's reverse the roles for a minute. Imagine: you need to do your grocery shopping. Upon entering the store, you are told you need your club card before you can buy anything. Lost it? You'll need to buy a new one. You can't use that shopping cart because someone else has it on hold. Can't find the bakery? You ought to look it up in the grocery food catalog. How soon would you go back to that store?

Sometimes library rules are difficult for customers to understand and navigate. People don't want to hear about rules. Once the guidelines are known, library navigation is simple, but until you learn the unique guidelines in public libraries, access is forbidding and off limits. Remember back to your own library training. It took a while just to understand how to search the catalog, then how to locate the item. It's quicker and easier for many customers to ask how to find something than to learn how to use the catalog. In addition, librarians uphold unique policies, penalties, and punishments: overdue and lost fines, claims returns, fees for holds that were not picked up, or lost library cards. Customers must learn how to place items on hold, how to place an interlibrary loan request, and figure out to which branch it will be delivered. Once the customer identifies the database, digital book, or physical book needed, more steps are needed to finally connect with the actual resource. Classification systems designed for library efficiency, such as Dewey Decimal, require customers to locate materials in a way that's familiar to library staff but not the consumer. Once the customer locates the book, she's faced with using the self-service machine. Experienced library staff understand how libraries work, but how much time and effort is a customer willing to invest in obtaining materials when there are so many obstacles in the way? How many customers have public libraries lost to retail businesses that can deliver unencumbered, friendly, and easy service? Personalized customer service may take from several seconds to several minutes, but it always ensures the library customer is supported through all of her information-seeking activities.

Providing good customer service is more than a rote activity limited to a generic smile and a welcome statement. How often have you heard, for example, "Welcome to (retail business). Today we have a special offer. If you buy one pair of jeans at the regular price, you'll get 50 percent off the second pair." Consumers are met with scripted greetings in order to increase the probability of a sale; however, when the identical phrase is repeated for each and every customer and delivered in the same unenthusiastic tone, the message becomes impersonal and monotonous. Customers are so accustomed to many rote greetings that they simply no longer listen. The same holds true in public libraries. It may not be the mechanical greeting that librarians are guilty of delivering, but how often do we think we know what someone needs before we are asked? We may think we're providing good customer service by anticipating the customer's needs, but sometimes we make assumptions before we fully understand the request. Based on our customer service experience, which stems from handling hundreds of requests, we think we are able to predict what the customer needs. Transactions based on anticipating customers' needs alone don't take into consideration the unique situations of customers' lives.

Top retail businesses seek to provide a welcoming and fun experience in order to make sales and establish customer loyalty. They connect with customers through a personalized approach. Throughout this book you'll read about retail businesses that provide models for delivering great service. I readily acknowledge that public libraries are not retail businesses, but read on: we can borrow winning business models, apply what works, and create our own model that's easy to provide and exceeds customer expectations.

Most traditional customer service training will probably be forgotten or disregarded in a few days or weeks. We often settle back into our habits because we've forgotten what we've learned; it's difficult to sustain the standards outlined in the training when it's formulaic and prescribed. Providing good customer service seems to come more naturally to some than others, but with suggestions in the chapters to come for new ways to connect with customers, everyone can achieve more layers of personalized service.

Successful businesses hire nice people! What has caused Starbucks, Zappos, and Amazon employees to exceed customer expectations for so many years? They've developed a culture of service in which it's okay to chat with customers and offer something extra on occasion—even when it falls outside of the rules. Imagine! These are staff who rarely receive customer complaints and who derive happiness from helping others.

Customer service standards must be reevaluated from time to time in light of today's savvy, spontaneous, and tech-oriented consumers. People want convenience and ease of service that specifically serves their unique wants and needs. Consumers will frequent businesses that provide consistent quality, variety, and good service; they will avoid shopping where their expectations aren't met. It's time for librarians to adopt a fresh new customer-centric model of service. When I say that libraries need to adopt a fresh new customer service model, I'm actually referring to all of us: those who are on the front lines, engaged in face-to-face interactions, and those in areas behind the front lines in various departments, administration, and other areas of public service.

I'd also like to clarify from the beginning that the term "librarian" in this book is used to describe any person who provides library service. Let's face it: customers refer to all of us as librarians—from director to shelver. We should accept and appreciate the recognition that the public affords us. Let's also address the term "library." The heart of this book focuses on public library work; however, only a slim difference exists between library types. All libraries serve the customer, whether the library is housed in a hospital, museum, university, corporation, or school. The service we provide is based on customer need, and our goals include making information available. Staff in public library service, however, encounter a broader swath of society, which expands our responsibility for creating a culture in which customer service thrives.

This book was created for you, librarians. We come in a variety of strengths, and no two are alike, which makes us uniquely prepared to take on the variety of questions asked. Unless you work in a library, are related to a librarian through friendship or kin, or spend a lot of time observing librarians, you probably have no idea of the number of talents and skills required to carry out the job. Librarians are dedicated to the mission of the library, and they are advocates of information and accessibility.

I think you'll agree that we are social workers, friends, advisers, supporters, confidants, negotiators, leaders, teachers, ambassadors, emergency workers, and consultants. We receive an array of questions from people of all ages and backgrounds that no other business, organization, or agency has the capacity to answer. Your unique experiences and challenges meeting needs are acknowledged in this book. The customer service you provide to your community will only be enhanced when practicing yes-focused customer service. Yes-focused customer service will make your job easier and sustain personal happiness.

Looking beyond library land, we'll learn that customer service excellence can be modeled from successful retail models. We'll look at the Nordstrom, Zappos, and Amazon models, which provide easy, stress-free, and positive customer experiences. Developed based on successful retail standards that increase sales and customer loyalty, *Yes! on Demand* breaks free from the stereotypical, shushing, rule-based library service rooted in "no." Library policies and procedures contain so many rules that librarians can lose site of the real mission of the library. Staff may rely on "no" responses because they are required to strictly follow policy and procedure, regardless of the effect on access. They feel that their role is to protect library assets, rather than looking at ways to extend access and build customer appreciation. Librarians must be empowered to negotiate "yes" decisions based on their own good judgment and experience. Staff must be trusted to make the right calls.

A practical guide for creating a personalized customer service experience, *Yes! on Demand* both acknowledges and leverages our greatest asset: library staff. We must believe that staff hold the power to shift public perception of libraries. Empowered, we will connect with the customer using our own talents, creativity, and strengths. We can break out of narrow, outdated, and restrictive practices and embrace a model that frees our customers and ourselves to create supportive and positive relationships.

In the following chapters you'll learn some of the reasons that libraries do not meet customer expectations and how customers view librarians and libraries, explore how libraries drive people away, and learn how to examine the attitudinal barriers that block customer service excellence. *Yes! on Demand* customer service ensures the relevance and the future of the public library in a culture that demands and expects service that exceeds expectations.

NOTE

1. Joseph R. Matthews, *The Customer-Focused Library: Re-Inventing the Public Library from the Outside-In* (Santa Barbara, CA: Libraries Unlimited, 2009), 12.

1

Heroes on the Front Line

People everywhere live with stress, and that's evident to librarians when library customers arrive at the service desk looking for solutions to life's challenges. Librarians work with people affected by poverty, disease, hunger, and loneliness, as well as those with criminal or other disturbing backgrounds. It's no wonder that stressors carried in by customers affect library staff. This chapter acknowledges the difficulties that librarians face in handling customer challenges and points to unpredictable situations that influence their capacity to respond effectively. Librarians listen, solve, and overall remain empathetic and unflappable, but over time their resilience can fade to harshness. In addition to acknowledging public library workers as heroes on the front line, this chapter addresses how to leverage stressors from the community outside to inform customer service strategies for staff on the inside.

WHAT PEOPLE DON'T KNOW ABOUT LIBRARY WORK

People ask the strangest questions. Few people outside the public library workforce realize the types of questions librarians grapple with each day. In an average week, most librarians will be faced with answering questions that affect a customer's emotional or physical well-being. Those of us on the inside, however, are not surprised at all. Questions library staff are asked range from easy fixes to all-out quests. The type of customer, like the questions asked, may range from safe and stable to irrational and downright scary. But despite the peculiarity and complexity of customer queries, most librarians possess an amazing capacity for maintaining incredible composure during these exchanges. Librarians quickly learn while serving at the desk to anticipate the unexpected and understand that absolutely anything can beat the previous day's surprising question. Let's also acknowledge that librarians face distractions that impede customer service—distractions that wear on staff over time.

Staff are first responders to fires, floods, and fistfights, jumping into action during emergencies and threats. The first to witness unlawful acts—drunkenness, sexual activity, drug deals, facility defacement, or graffiti—librarians on the front lines take quick and decisive action. They show concern for and regularly check on those who are asleep to make sure they're not sick, unconscious, or worse. Something as simple as waking up a customer can easily escalate into a full-blown incident, depending on the customer's condition. Waking up customers creates its own surprises, depending on the customer's physical and cognitive state when roused. Staff approach such customers bravely, albeit with a measure of caution.

Librarians are the first to sniff out unusual odors to discover and eliminate the source. Arson in restrooms, electrical malfunctions, or the unknown—librarians jump into action for everyone's safety. Body odors, the foulest of all, must also be addressed by valiant library staff, who understand that it's the right of both staff and the public to enjoy a relatively odor-free environment. When library customers complain about a visitor's odor, staff are expected to decide if the odor warrants expulsion or not. Even when staff and customers are seen scattering from the odor's source, it doesn't make delivering the message to the stinky customer any easier.

Unattended children, the innocent victims of abandonment, present another common challenge for public library staff to address. Too young to be left in the library alone for hours, children naturally look to librarians to satisfy their physical or emotional hunger, or both. Excuses given by caregivers who've left young children unattended include: "I was just going to run to the store and right back"; "During the summer my kids live in the library"; and "His sister was supposed to be watching him." Often the caregiver offers no excuse at all but blames library staff for bringing up the concern and suggesting the parent act responsibly. Library personnel must determine when to search for the parent, seek the help of law enforcement, or contact child protective services. Attention to abandoned children requires time and patience from library staff, who seek to maintain a balance between customer service and customer protection.

Librarians, like doctors and clergy, listen to customers without judging. It's not unusual for public librarians to meet people in life crises that require immediate attention, and they frequently hear: "I need a place to stay tonight," or "I need food." Librarians provide a huge service for the community by referring people with life needs to local resources and agencies that can help. Because people realize that librarians are trustworthy sources of information, some also wander in from the streets looking for answers to every manner of life problem. Because of stressors tied to finding work, food, or shelter, it's not uncommon for library customers to fall apart emotionally at the information desk in response to answers that don't fill their needs. People frustrated with government resources, online applications, and other bureaucratic processes may ask a librarian for help because the library represents free access and knowledge for all. But because of the stressors associated with life's trials, librarians receive verbal and—less often—physical abuse. When a customer's level of frustration exceeds their ability to cope, librarians will face the fallout.

It's amazing the extent to which customers trust librarians to keep information confidential. Desperate life needs are often revealed during the reference interview and frequently begin with self-help information requests. For example, I remember staffing a busy information desk when a woman with a bruised cheek asked for books on spousal abuse. So there I was, faced with the choice of providing her with her exact request or offering her more, all based on the conclusion I'd drawn from the bruise on her face and her question. Because our library worked closely with the county crisis center, a supply of crisis hotline business cards was kept on the counter. I grabbed a card from the desk, walked her to the stacks, and after sharing a few books with her, gave her the card. I told her that a call to the crisis center would connect her with even more resources than the public library had on hand. If I was wrong about how I had interpreted the bruise on her face, she didn't let on, and she accepted the card.

Not all people in crises expect to find solutions at the public library, but many will find the answers they need with staff who are open to listening for cues that point to the root problem. It's not unusual for customers to share their innermost fears, such as recent medical diagnoses or struggles with addiction or depression. Librarians also provide answers for people's most frightening situations: cancer, alcoholism, and abusive relationships (see table 1.1). I remember another example, when I helped a customer locate material about a terminal diagnosis she'd just been given. Even though librarians cannot provide medical advice, they know they will be asked. Because customers trust the advice offered by librarians along with the reputation the library represents, customers may share deeply personal stories with staff at the desk. Conversations that customers hesitate to engage in with friends or family may land on the public library desk.

Due to the governmental bureaucracy with which many of our libraries are associated, customers may perceive staff as perpetrators in a grand scheme to capture their money through fines and take away their individual freedom to act however they want in the library. Are you familiar with the following statements? "I pay you. You government workers are all alike—you're lazy and have bad attitudes," or "All you do is sit on your fat lazy butt all day." Although it seems unfair to accuse library staff of being lazy or dumb, angry or upset patrons are not usually offended by any particular staff member but by what she or he represents: a big, audacious government machine. Steve Albrecht, library security expert, summarizes how to quit taking it personally (QTIP): "Most of the time, angry or entitled patrons

Table 1.1.   Common Stressors, Needs, and Conversations

Stressor	Need	Words Customers Use
Job loss Bankruptcy Low wages Single parent Homeless Finances	Food Shelter Job Money	Résumé Job board Computer help Grants Civil service test books Job Shelters Food bank Child care Help Bankruptcy/legal resources Collectible/antiques values

Domestic abuse
Dysfunctional
  home
Broken
  relationship
Family crisis
	Divorce/separation
	Emancipation for
	  minors
	Shelter
	Rape crisis
	  intervention
	Law enforcement
	Grief counseling
		Relationship self-help
		Books recently mentioned on daytime
		  TV programs, radio news shows
		Doctor or psychologist in media
		Spousal abuse resources
		Divorce resources
		Books by psychics
		Religious books
		Programs for teens

Physical/emotional conditions	Addiction Codependency Medical Psychological Grief	Relationship self-help Medical resources List of doctors and hospitals Religion Healer Psychic

Disease, disability,
  and pain
	Medical books,
	  journals
	Medical resources/
	  referral
		Nutrition
		PDR
		Referral to crisis center or crisis
		  phone number
		Specific disease
		Homeopathy
		Diet books
		Cookbooks
		ADA law

Citizenship	Citizenship classes Job Community resources	Language learning resources Testing materials Citizenship books/resources English conversation groups Community college Adult education Technology classes High school classes

aren't mad at you personally; they're mad at what you represent—a public space entity with rules, a code of conduct, and policies they find irritating, chafing, or not meant for them."[1] Even so, when staff bear the brunt of verbal or physical abuse, it's difficult to remain emotionally unreactive. In my ten years of library experience, I've personally known coworkers who have been punched, slapped, kicked, shoved up against walls, followed, ogled, and spat on. Others have been cornered in the elevator, threatened with assault, and, regrettably, beaten and hospitalized.

Library Incidents

As we've read, heroes on the front lines meet customers looking for answers to life stressors. They facilitate finding food and shelter; direct customers to medical resources; and address disruptions thwarting the intended use of the library, whether due to criminal activity, facility destruction, or odor issues. The following discussion drills down to specific library incidents and how they affect staff ability to provide a positive customer experience. Most customer service books tend to focus on rational customer responses, without considering the number of irrational customers visiting our public libraries.

Dealing with incidents begins with an internal alarm that a customer's glare, mannerisms, or words have deteriorated into pre-incident behaviors. When this thought goes through our minds—"This customer just asked me an irrational question," or "This person just reacted badly to the answer I provided"—staff should abandon trying to answer the original question the customer asked and instead focus on how to manage what may develop into an incident. For instance, a customer may shout: "You sent me to the collection agency and I expect you to take that fine off of my account right now!"; or "The government is after me and the man at Computer 12 is part of the conspiracy"; or "My doctor and my family don't believe me. I have a disease caused by a parasite that invaded my body. I can see it on my skin but no one else can." Front-line staff need to switch gears into incident management mode. This requires focusing on the customer's behavior only and how to end the transaction safely and quickly. This is the other side of customer service that is seldom discussed. Library staff need to protect other customers' right to enjoy the library. Disruptions provide staff with opportunities to resolve concerns that detract from a positive library experience. Library security experts who've dedicated much of their life's work to teaching staff how to respond to incidents agree that incidents must be addressed quickly and consistently.

Currently, no single source collects information on the number of public library incidents in the United States, but library leadership and staff know they occur frequently. Having worked in two large library systems, I have handled incidents numbering in the hundreds. In this chapter I review library incidents from urban libraries and consider responses to a poll conducted with library leaders who were willing to share their statistics. Reaching out to the respondents resulted in my requesting additional information about security choices—law enforcement or private—and the amount budgeted for library security. Library incident management is a growing concern in public libraries, especially when we consider the number of books and amount of training provided on the subjects of security, "difficult" customers, and stress in the workplace. A great deal of time, attention, and resources are being spent on incidents that begin in routine customer service transactions.

As a result of finding only scattered published reports of public library incidents in articles and newspapers, I created a poll and invited participants on the Urban Libraries Council (ULC) and California Library Information Exchange (CALIX) to provide answers. Ten libraries quickly responded to the following questions:

1. What is the name of your library? The name of your library will not be published, but it will be helpful to know your library size and other statistics.
2. Does your library or library system have security officers in one or more locations?
3. How many total incidents did your library document in FY 2014–2015?
4. How many incidents involved patron misconduct?
5. How many incidents required banning a patron for a period of six months or longer?
6. How many incidents required a permanent ban?
7. Other comments:
8. May I contact you if I have follow-up questions? My contact information:

Follow-up question:

9. To follow up on the survey you took regarding the number of incidents at your library in 2014–2015, would you also be able to provide any security costs?

All but one library responded "Yes" to the question, "Does your library or library system have security officers in one or more locations?" The number of library locations ranged from one library with four incidents and no security to nine large library systems, all requiring on-site security. The highest number of incidents involving patron misconduct was 880 during FY 2014–2015, and all libraries reported incidents involving some type of patron misconduct (see table 1.2).

The sampling of responses from California to Kentucky indicates that the majority of libraries polled hire off-duty law enforcement officers or private security companies to assist in incidents. This is a hefty price tag for public libraries to bear, but tangential to this discussion is the need to acknowledge that front-line staff also bear the load of incident management. We can look to the number of library security books written, and the amount of "difficult

Table 1.2. Library Incidents

	Respondent 1	Respondent 2	Respondent 3	Respondent 4	Respondent 5	Respondent 6	Respondent 7	Respondent 8	Respondent 9	Respondent 10
Q1	CA 1–10 locations	TX 1–10 locations	KY 11–20 locations	CA 50+ locations	CA 21–49 locations	MO 21–49 locations	CA 50+ locations	MI 1–10 locations	KY 1–10 locations	CA 21–49 locations
Q2	Yes	No	Yes	Yes	Yes	Yes	Yes	Yes	Yes	Yes
Q3	150	4	880	1110	440	362	797	124	541	530
Q4	75	4	880	322	375	131	447	124	541	465
Q5	5	0	80	0	0	3	13	25	42	unknown
Q6	5	0	80	0	0	3	13	25	42	
Q7	No response	Minor incident, sleeping	No response	No response	Ability to ban started FY14–15	Majority of incidents occur at 6 locations, 4 have off-duty police	No response	Will send documents	No response	
Q8	Yes	Yes	Yes	Yes	Yes	Yes	Yes	Yes	Yes	Yes
Q9	$379,224 Library contracts with county sheriff	n/a	$267,000			$280,000		$58,000 security provided by private security; wear suits, no weapons		

and challenging" patron training available, to realize that library incidents do impact staff ability to provide excellent and consistent customer service. Here I explore how to provide yes-focused customer service despite getting sidetracked by incident management, as well as how we can support each other in doing so.

In the Spotlight

The Toledo-Lucas (OH) County Public Library captured public attention when an article titled "Trouble Often Shatters Hush of Local Libraries" was published in the *Blade* newspaper in January 2015.[2] The story described patron behaviors in the library's nearly one thousand incidents per year between 2012 and 2015 throughout its nineteen buildings, sharing the library's problems with criminal and sexual activity, theft, vandalism, and Internet pornography. This type of customer behavior is not unusual in public libraries across the United States, and the response here is a collective "I hear you" and recognition that any public library is subject to the press's investigative scrutiny.

Security reports requested from Toledo-Lucas County Public Library, along with interviews conducted by the newspaper, resulted in a published account of the library customers' challenging behaviors. The downtown library location of Toledo-Lucas County reported seventy-four cases of disruptive behavior and harassment against staff members and patrons in 2014. The library's code of conduct at the time of publication was enforced by staff along with twenty-two armed security officers and eight off-duty sheriff's deputies, who worked for the library and its branches. Staff members reported dealing with quite a few instances of harassment and regularly scanned public computer use for pornography while on duty.

Infractions there resulted in a library ban for one week for viewing pornography, and up to one year when viewing was accompanied by sexual activity. It was also reported that security guards regularly search for intoxicated people. Staff must also be on alert for people carrying weapons into the library. In summary, the Toledo-Lucas County Library became the subject of a newspaper investigation in which security reports were shared with the community, which overshadowed any positive outcomes the library provided for the community. The attention on Toledo-Lucas County Library reminded public library administrators and staff everywhere of the enormity of the social problems that appear in public libraries. We work in situations in which we must remain alert and act responsibly for the protection of staff and the public so we can focus on providing resources that lead to meaningful outcomes.

Overwhelming as it seems, library incidents can be managed effectively by adopting the precepts shared by security experts, which includes taking swift action in addressing incidents. Admittedly, incident management isn't what drew us into public library work, but the customers engaged in triggering incidents block information access for all others. It takes courage to lead the charge in managing library incidents, as Albrecht discusses: "Courage is a learned skill, and one I admire. I like library directors with the courage to do the right thing, and I have seen many examples of this. They take ownership and defend their right to create a safe, functioning, peaceful place to work and visit."[3] Evicting or banning customers who disrupt library service will tell your staff and customers that they are valued and supported. Those who disrupt library service should be swiftly removed and, when appropriate, banned from ever reentering.

Disruptive Behavior and Setting Boundaries

The U.S. Department of Labor, Occupational Safety and Health Administration (OSHA) publishes workplace violence risk factors that librarians should be aware of but definitely not obsess over. Workplace violence is defined as "any act or threat of physical violence, harassment, intimidation, or other threatening disruptive behavior that occurs at the work site. It ranges from threats and verbal abuse to physical assaults and even homicide. It can affect and involve employees, clients, customers and visitors."[4] Library staff engage in nine of the twelve activities that increase the risk of violence in the workplace: (1) exchanging money with the public; (2) working with volatile, unstable people; (3) working alone or in isolated areas; (4) providing services and care; (5) working where alcohol is served; (6) working late at night or in areas with high crime rates; (7) exchanging money with delivery drivers; (8) practicing health care; (9) being public service workers; (10) being customer service agents; (11) being law enforcement personnel; and finally, (12) working alone or in small groups.[5] With the exception of serving alcohol, practicing health care, and enforcing the law, librarians fall into most of these categories. Staff should be aware of some of the factors that may trigger negative customer responses. Taking the stance of zero tolerance in the form of consistent policies and their enforcement, in order to curtail illegal, violent, or disruptive behavior, will set the stage for providing yes-focused customer service, the best service imaginable.

In addition to providing consistent policies and practices that protect everyone in the library, staff need to receive support as they deal with incidents. *HealthDay* newsletter, written by Richard Bermack, gives a nod to librarians who face challenging incidents, not only to acknowledge the challenges but also to recognize the need for self-care. In "Librarians Under Siege," Bermack describes public library work as risky for staff at Berkeley Public Library, who became the focus of his article.[6] Librarians there regularly manage a number of challenging patron behaviors stemming from mental illness and other stressors associated with homelessness and financial challenges. An unstable homeless woman crossed the line when her behavior escalated from threatening language, which intimidated staff, to kicking and punching at a librarian. Swift action resulted in a restraining order being taken out that will protect both staff and the public. Berkeley Public librarians help with resources such as shelter, food, or other life services as part of their regular duties. With the library receiving at least thirty homeless people daily, much of their work is focused on incident management and social service support. Like librarians across America, they stand in the cross fire of aggression and compassion, judging when to help and when to run.

Heroes in Tumultuous Times

Ferguson Municipal Public Library opened its doors the morning after a violent night of protests resulting from a Missouri grand jury's decision not to indict the white police officer who fatally shot African American teen Michael Brown. Scott Bonner, library director at Ferguson Municipal Public Library, wanted to provide a safe place for children to visit while the public schools remained closed. While others were saying *no* by keeping their businesses boarded up, Bonner bravely took a stand, erring on the side of access, despite the potential for further incidents. Though many businesses in the area hunkered down and locked their doors, Bonner decided the best way to serve the community was to stay open. The library provided a safe place in which to host activities for Ferguson's kids and became a haven for children dealing with the emotional trauma tearing the community apart.[7] In Berry's *Courage in Crisis*, Bonner describes his reasons for remaining focused on yes and eliminating no: "I've done a lot of thinking about the library's mission and how broadly we can define it so that I can say 'yes,' and not be gatekeeping and stopping things. I want to say 'yes' to everything I can. We're going to run the library too hot, things are going to break. Things are going to go sideways. I'd rather do too much and have things go sideways than do too little."[8] Scott Bonner is a library hero on the front lines. Ferguson Municipal Public Library was awarded Library of the Year 2015 by Gale/*Library Journal*.

Although safety is required for a positive public library experience, the amount of time and energy required to manage incidents has certainly increased over the years. Security experts are summoned to our libraries to lead training and conduct security audits, while the number of incidents grows. Steve Albrecht notes that libraries "will have to deal with the changing nature of patrons today, which means more mental illness with some of them, more substance abuse, more kids with behavior problems—left alone in the library by parents who leave them for hours—and plenty of boundary-pushing behaviors by the entitled, who don't believe your rules or codes of conduct ever apply to them."[9] Listen to patrons and staff when they report that they are afraid. They have a valid reason. Patrons who behave badly will likely repeat the behavior, and if no consequences are imposed by the library, the bad behavior will not improve and may even worsen.[10] Taking steps to confront the source of incidents requires consistency, but the effort will confirm your library's commitment to safety for the public and your staff.

Dealing with library incidents requires an incredible amount of staff time. Writing up a report, submitting it, and any post-incident follow-ups drain staff energy and the library's precious financial resources. Workplace incidents restrict the mission of the public library and must be managed judiciously. Major incidents are often precipitated by previous ones, which suggests that public library staff should make an effort to address incidents while they are relatively minor before they develop into full-blown bad situations.

I once woke up to a blaring fire alarm in my fifteenth-floor apartment, only to hear the intercom voice saying, "Don't be alarmed. We have a minor incident that we are dealing with." No incident is minor if alarms and announcements wake up residents at 2:00 am. Unmanaged incidents open the door to future, more intensely challenging incidents. There are no minor incidents. All need attention. Writing incident reports temporarily distracts staff ability to provide front-line customer service. Report writing may take from ten minutes to hours, based on the complexity of the incident and the number of people involved. There is little research available on the number of incidents recorded in public libraries across America, but it can be assumed from the random sampling of large and small public libraries discussed above that library incidents cost millions of dollars each year and dilute funding strength for programs and services that enhance people's lives. Managing library incidents communicates your library's commitment to yes-focused customer service.

Emotional Impact

Difficult public library encounters cannot be avoided, and not surprisingly, many library staff members will be involved in an incident at some time during their careers. Incidents occur in a surprising variety of forms, delivered by a host of assailants. They are unprovoked and occur regularly or without warning; they take a toll on front-line staff who try to make sense of it all, replaying the incident over in their minds to see what they could have done differently. Repetitive, intentionally destructive acts affect library staff; these maladaptive behaviors are directed at either the facility, security personnel, library customers, or staff. Whether chronic or situational, many library customers arrive with problems such as homelessness, intoxication, mental disorders, or in an angry or agitated state.

Amazingly, most librarians are ready to return to their posts shortly after an incident, whether due to their deep sense of responsibility or because returning to work will provide a distraction from the incident. Steve Albrecht suggests taking time to reflect and debrief after incidents and shares the following about rules for safety, security, and service: "After a particularly difficult patron situation, debrief, support, and praise one another, when it's safe to do so."[11] Post-incident talks allow staff to share what's on their minds and work together to make improvements to the handling of incidents. When front-line staff talk with each other after incidents, they are better prepared to handle subsequent events. Particularly stressful incidents result in staff feeling scared, unsure, and often unsupported. When staff replay an incident with each other, they confirm and validate their actions and responses. When library leadership promotes debriefing, staff will feel supported and prepared to handle the next challenge. In addition to debriefing, there are ways to improve the way staff respond to incidents: "1) Use the power of your colleagues to work as a team on particularly difficult patron situations; and 2) Get outside help, support, and advice if necessary, especially from your stakeholders in safety and security (police or sheriff's department, HR, city attorney, county counsel, risk management personnel, facilities staff)."[12] Human resources departments may offer employee assistance program counselors for staff to consult; this is an invaluable resource for staff, and they should be encouraged to use it. Library incidents drain staff emotionally. Despite library administrators' best efforts to provide a safe and pleasant library experience, incidents will occur, and staff will bear the emotional fallout.

A library colleague who used to work in a library plagued by a high number of incidents, along with slow (or no) police response and absence of on-site security, took employees' well-being into her own hands. Procedures for handling incidents were clearly communicated and reviewed at my colleague's staff meetings. Debriefings were held after particularly trying incidents. Staff felt supported despite a number of horrendous incidents, including a patron's attempted suicide in the library bathroom, an assault on a staff member that required hospitalization, and numerous verbal assaults and threats of bodily harm to staff. This library manager not only equipped staff to deal with incidents but she also created a safe place for staff to psychologically recuperate after particularly stressful events. Staff were encouraged to debrief and review incidents in the breakroom. The safety of the breakroom decompression zone acknowledged the amount of emotional stress that staff bore and their supervisor's emphasis on self-care. Staff found a place to retreat and find solace despite the tension playing out in the library and surrounding community. A period to relax, play a game, or briefly watch TV offered a buffer between one incident and the next. The library's employee assistance program was utilized by staff for support beyond what supervisors or peers could provide.

Deanna's Story

I am not sure what I expected when I took my first supervisor position. The library was located in a busy low-income/high-crime neighborhood. I had been warned to expect numerous incidents and staff complaints, but nothing could have prepared me. I purposely, and perhaps foolishly, did not read past incident reports or staff performance reviews. I wanted to come into the location with fresh eyes.

It was clear that staff were eager to share their experiences of incidents. I met with them individually and listened to their concerns. No doubt staff were stressed and did not trust the leadership of an outsider. I had an open door policy. I wanted to understand what they were dealing with, which meant I needed to make myself available at all times to step in and help with challenging situations. I wanted staff to understand that I was a partner. A good and fair supervisor is one who would not ask staff to do something that she would be too afraid of dealing with herself.

After a few weeks, I recognized that I was stressed. I could only imagine what staff were feeling after several years working in this library. I openly admitted my concerns with staff and with my supervisor. Something needed to change! I needed staff to feel supported. Their well-being was my priority, and I repeatedly let them know that. I started by giving staff permission to allow themselves to be upset after dealing with stressful situations or challenging patrons. Staff had been worried that they would somehow get in trouble or be seen as weak if they allowed their feelings to show in any form. That was just adding to their stress. I recommended they take a moment to decompress in a safe place after an incident. I asked that staff come get me to relieve them on desk if they needed time to regroup and to rely on each other the same way if I wasn't there.

During meetings, I would reiterate the importance of self-care and ask staff to let me know what they needed to ease stress. Staff did not feel safe walking in the neighborhood, and there wasn't a place close by to escape, so we made the staff room a "no work" zone. It was a safe place to sit quietly without interruption. If a staff member was in the room on break, messages were taken and work discussions were placed on hold. We all agreed to enforce this rule. I also encouraged staff to find other ways to de-stress. We would play music in the staff area before we opened. I encouraged staff to listen to music on their earphones at their desks during their breaks. One staff member began meditating in the dark of the office during breaks. Another would bring a portable game console and play games during breaks or take a board game out to the public area and play with some of the kids in the library. I also forced staff to leave work at work. There was no need to take it home. Nothing was more important than their well-being.

We also began to look at what factors were leading to incidents. We acknowledged that many of our patrons were dealing with great outside stresses. Our patrons were struggling with low income, unstable home life, hunger, and fear of real violence on the streets. Several gang-related shootings occurred in the neighborhood. Fights and drug deals were visible from the front door of the library. By better understanding what our patrons were walking into the library with, we developed a higher level of empathy. Although being treated rudely or being pulled into an incident was not acceptable, it did relieve some of the pressure we placed on ourselves to keep the peace. Just acknowledging the elephant in the room, that our library was a tough place to work and we were only human, was a huge relief. The lessons I have to share:

1. Listen to staff needs.
2. Put yourself in staff shoes.
3. Lead from the front lines, not from the back office.
4. Admit when there is a problem.
5. Find solutions as a team; enforce them as a leader.
6. Acknowledge that there are things beyond your control and accept them for what they are.

When library supervisors and leadership openly recognize that staff need support for emotional well-being and put coping tools in place, the entire team will be bolstered. Staff need such support for emotional well-being, so put tools in place for their care. They will respond by providing outstanding service to others.

The scenarios listed above are just a few of the very real incidents faced in public libraries today. We must support each other so that we can better serve those who look to us for a vast number of information needs. Fortunately, the majority of customer interactions are pleasant and do not require debriefing and self-care, but challenging patron incidents must be acknowledged before embarking on *Yes! on Demand* customer service.

There are many more positive customer interactions than negative. In contrast to the negative experiences, librarians help children find that special book or share the fun of Summer Reading activities. Librarians award prizes; lead story-times; and bring children joy with songs, reading, and play. Librarians connect with children and people of all ages and backgrounds and care about people in the library community. They bring joy and happiness to customers, and customers often reciprocate. What observations have brought you delight or touched you in an emotional way? For me, it's seeing a young girl enjoying a subsidized summer lunch as she imagines the possibilities contained in the colorful books that surround her or overhearing a young adult slowly sounding out a simple word by the side of his literacy tutor. Working with teens provides momentary glimpses into their exclusive world of online gaming victories or dreams for the future. Public library work presents opportunities to experience fear, happiness, and bewilderment—regularly!

Through it all—the accusations, threats, and stressors we encounter—staff continue to serve the public every day and believe that the public library has the ability to change lives. The instances in which we are thanked for our help outweigh all of the negative experiences we encounter. Customers put a smile on our faces, and children have the unique ability to realign us with our original mission, especially when they state requests like, "I need a book about fish that live in the desert."

Librarians are the heroes of public library service and must be recognized as the library's most effective resource. They deserve accolades for their dedication to serving people. Trust, support, and acknowledgment for library staff as the heroes of the front line are the beginning of staff empowerment, which is the key to delivering yes-focused customer service.

NOTES

1. Steve Albrecht, "Better Communication, Safer Facilities," *American Libraries Magazine* 46 (September/October 2015): 52.

2. Ignazio Messina, "Trouble Often Shatters Hush of Local Libraries," *Blade* (Toledo, OH), January 4, 2015, http://www.toledoblade.com/local/2015/01/04/Trouble -often-shatters-hush-of-local-libraries.html.

3. Steve Albrecht, *Library Security: Better Communication, Safer Facilities* (Chicago: ALA Editions, 2015), xi.

4. United States Department of Labor, "What Is Workplace Violence?," https:// www.osha.gov/SLTC/workplaceviolence.

5. Ibid.

6. Richard Bermack, "Librarians Under Siege," *HealthDay*, January 20, 2015, http://consumer.healthday.com/encyclopedia/work-and-health-41/occupational -health-news-507/librarians-under-siege-646477.html.

7. John N. Berry III, "Courage in Crisis," *Library Journal* 140, no. 11 (June 15, 2015): 30.

8. Ibid.

9. Albrecht, *Library Security*, 3.

10. Ibid., 20.

11. Ibid.

12. Ibid.

2

Shift in Thinking Required

Heroes on the front line, as we discussed in chapter 1, face challenges that affect staff's ability to deliver consistent and positive customer service. This chapter focuses on the challenges library leaders face in striving to create a culture of service for both staff and customers. We study, compare, and contrast how for-profit business leaders achieve that culture. Customer service excellence depends on leadership's ability to create a positive culture that encourages staff participation: one that provides hope, encouragement, and support. *Yes! on Demand* customer service will take root when leaders focus on creating a culture immersed in trust. This chapter describes the degree to which internal customer service directly affects external customer service and how both are inextricably linked.

Yes! on Demand customer service starts with leadership. Library directors initiate the ultimate "yes" environment by modeling positive customer service with staff and the public and by eliminating the confines of hierarchical structure. Great library leaders love to engage with customers wherever they are, and their infectious fervor for all things library inspires staff on the front line. The best leaders genuinely care about customers and provide personalized service by listening to suggestions from the public as well as concerns raised by staff. In looking to business models rather than peer libraries alone, we can learn how customer service infiltrates every area of business and, ultimately, library success.

The most successful business leaders in the world recognize the power of their employees not only to sustain but also to exponentially increase them. The decisions that library staff make when they are trusted inspire them to use their winning personal skills, which bring delight to customers. Lou Gerstner, who initiated positive change in IBM culture, shared that the attitudes and behaviors of large organizations are very difficult to achieve and cannot be mandated, engineered, or declared by leadership. "You can define the marketplace realities and goals. But then you have to trust. In fact, in the end, management doesn't change culture. Management invites the work-force itself to change the culture. Perhaps the toughest nut of all to crack was getting IMB employees to accept that invitation."[1] A shift in library culture will occur when staff are given hope, encouragement, and support. Because culture relies on the people inside the organization to act, leader-ship can only create the environment, step back, and allow staff to test the waters of change.

CULTURE OF HOPE, ENCOURAGEMENT, AND SUPPORT

Hope

Strong leadership and empowered staff create hope and encourage trust in the library between leadership and staff. Hope is the expectation that something good will happen. It drives people into action, inspiring them to stay the course and set their sights on the future. Staff will thrive within a hopeful environment. When planning and implementing new ideas, listen to staff suggestions. Not only do they want to be involved, but their input is essential for all of the elements needed to create a customer service culture. Coordinate work groups for special projects based on library goals. Develop healthy teams that thrive on participation in plans; give team members time to bond at the beginning and the freedom to share openly and without fear. Invite staff who have traditionally been unenthusiastic or unengaged to par-ticipate in a project to which they can contribute a particular talent, skill, or interest in learning more.

Frontline staff are often expected to deliver new types of service despite never being invited into the discussion or given the reasons for change. Library staff should be included in all of the decisions that affect their ability to deliver exceptional customer service. Staff are experts at anticipating bar-riers and loopholes in proposed changes, and their feedback bolsters any transition in new products or services. Listen to staff concerns and respond. Staff know more about what customers are saying and how they are react-ing to new products and services than anyone else, but they are the least likely to be consulted. Their participation as consultants on the front line will ensure that a culture of service permeates the entire organization.

World-Renowned Leadership

Staff participation in organizational development requires the elimination of hierarchical barriers and release of control over them. Every leader is unique, but there are shared qualities that great leaders possess. Libraries at-tract a wide swath of people from a variety of educational and experiential backgrounds, and the most interesting, intelligent thinkers and doers any-where work in public libraries. Library staff share an affinity for knowing how to retrieve the best resources for their customers and, not surprisingly, for themselves. Because libraries attract so many types of learners and doers, the initial interest in working for a library could soon diminish if leadership does not offer a deeper meaning and fulfillment that inspires a commitment to the vision, mission, and goals of the library. Long-term staff satisfaction is determined by leadership's ability to engage staff in participating across the entire organization.

Continually breaking with hierarchal structures, Richard Branson (best known for founding the Virgin Group, which you may remember as Virgin Records or Virgin Megastores) created a culture of service by leveling out organizational hierarchy. He gave each employee ownership of the company philosophy.

Employees are valued and acknowledged. Branson's amazing capacity to deliver what the customer wants in all of his businesses drives his decisions down to the last detail and ultimately increases profits. Library leaders can learn from entrepreneurs like Branson, who base their organizational structure on staff empowerment and trust, with more of a philosophical approach. When asked what it takes to generate a healthy level of staff engagement, Branson responded: "In my opinion it comes down to strong leadership and developing a culture in which your employees feel valued, empowered and trusted."[2] Regardless of the type of business, for-profit or not, leaders who create thriving businesses recognize the power that staff wield to keep the business growing and strong.

Branson criticizes a business culture that overemphasizes "knowing your position" and argues that it can actually result in interfering with progress and innovation.[3] Keeping staff and leaders in a box closes off possibilities for support and growth. Let's imagine all of the library staff duties within a Venn diagram. Our goal should be to increase the common areas that overlap. Suggesting that multiple layers of leadership are found in "healthy, results-oriented rather than status-conscious structures,"[4] Branson encourages staff at every level to fully participate. Multilayered leadership fosters a culture of customer service by providing staff with hope that their ideas are respected and considered.

When employees are trusted, they not only support leadership, they freely speak up for change and create new ways of solving problems. Characteristics of remarkable leaders, many of whom built multi-million-dollar businesses based on creating ultimate customer experiences, are extrapolated below into a replicable platform for libraries. Delivering excellent customer service is one of the primary duties of library staff, and the extent to which it's enthusiastically delivered depends on the degree of trust given by leaders. Transactions based in finding the "yes" solution rather than "no" begin with trusting staff to make good decisions for the customer, sometimes outside of formulaic boundaries. Library administrators who empower library teams and staff to work independently under conditions free of harsh criticism will be free to focus on activities that strengthen the library. As a result, staff who are trusted will focus their attention on customer needs rather than on restrictions that bind their ability to make thoughtful decisions for the customer. Trusting staff cannot be accomplished by leadership without releasing some control to others. When staff have little or no control of their work environment, they suffer more stress on the job. When a leader is dominant or controlling, the staff's voices will be diminished.

Fred Smith, founder of Federal Express (now FedEx Corporation), commented on looking for the right people to work at FedEx: "I have often said it's better to ask forgiveness than permission. It requires everybody out there making decisions at whatever level."[5] Smith realized that company success is directly related to staff who are empowered to think on their own and are unafraid to make decisions. Likewise, Nordstrom empowers its staff to "act like entrepreneurs to satisfy the customer."[6] Imagine being empowered to think of the library as a library director or shop owner would. Customer service is transformed when staff take ownership of their transactions. They begin to think in terms of the library's future, the health of the organization, future plans, innovative ideas, ways to improve service, and empathy for the customer's library experience. In contrast, when staff fear they will be in trouble with their supervisor if they waive a fine, extend borrowing time, or take a few extra minutes to help someone, the customer experience naturally suffers. What opportunities are lost when staff are not backed up by a supportive supervisor or library administration to do what's necessary to provide an outstanding customer experience? Staff excel at providing customer service when granted the freedom to problem solve in favor of the customer, without the fear of reprisal. Allow staff to use their own good judgment for problem solving. What harm can come from allowing library customers to gain improved access to library materials and services? Notable library leaders encourage creativity and allow staff to make mistakes. The very best library leaders admit their own mistakes and trust staff to make the right decisions.

Lack of Control and Stress

Simon Sinek's *Leaders Eat Last* provides an insightful journey into the biological responses to stress that the human body retains from millennia ago. The types of stress encountered in our working environments today are very different from the flight and fight days, but biological responses remain the same while managing stress. Sinek describes today's work environments as tending "to be full of cynicism, paranoia and self-interest."[7] One would presume that a leader's stress level is higher than that of subordinates, but Sinek argues that this is not the case. Researchers in the Whitehall Studies found that stress in the workplace was not associated with higher rank or responsibility, but rather the "degree of control workers feel they have throughout the day."[8] Sinek concluded that staff who feel that they have less control of their work environment feel more stress.[9] Another study in 2012, conducted by Harvard and Stanford researchers, looked at cortisol (stress hormone) levels and found that leaders have lower stress levels than their employees.[10] It's a fascinating study, because library leaders often think they have the highest level of stress of anyone in the library, but in fact, those who work on the front lines do. Staff must often accept the fact that they have little control over decisions made by library leadership. It is that lack of control over employees' work and their lives that causes stress, Sinek hypothesizes. Looking at this study strictly from a health perspective provides reason enough to speculate, as Sinek does, that a supportive workplace supports good health: "Those who feel they have more control, who feel empowered to make decisions instead of waiting for approval, suffer less stress. Those only doing as they are told, always forced to follow the rules, are the ones who suffer most. Feelings of control, stress, and the ability to perform at a high level, are all directly tied to how safe we feel in our organizations."[11] The more control over customer service transactions leadership allows, the less stress staff will encounter. Leaders who trust staff to make decisions will be rewarded by workers who are engaged and committed to the library philosophy.

Trust

Sir Terry Leahy, former CEO of Tesco, shares the importance of trust in the workplace under effective leadership: "If I had to sum it up, it would be about being generous at work rather than selfish. And it is amazing how often you see people who can't help themselves, because of their ambition or their insecurities or whatever—that they're basically selfish and they take rather than give. . . . Sometimes the brightest find it the hardest to make that transition because they've always been better than the people around them. They find it hard to trust the people around them to do the work."[12] Leahy asserts that organizations struggle because leaders cannot trust others whom they perceive as being less smart or overly ambitious or some other insecurity. Creating conditions, Leahy describes, "where people can work together because they trust each other . . . empowers the organization."[13] In theory, trust is a simple concept, but in practice it's sometimes difficult to let go of control. Leaders will always benefit from sharing responsibilities with the people who want to do the best for the library. Trusted employees make leaders shine.

Hiring the right people guarantees that *Yes! on Demand* service is delivered. Personalized service can be delivered during a five-second or a fifteen-minute transaction. Personalized service and customized service is the focus here, not so much the amount of time spent. Imagine a customer who finally musters up courage to ask a librarian for books about spousal abuse, or the grandmother who asks for help finding her reading tutor for the first time, or the unemployed person asking for résumé or job-searching help. If customers with the greatest needs are met by surly or rushed staff, it's likely the customer's needs will go unmet. In addition to these examples, hundreds of other scenarios exist that illustrate the amount of trust customers place in librarians. When staff remain courteous, doors of possibility open that provide opportunities for life-changing customer interactions. The underused term "courteousness" should be an expectation for staff in all public libraries and be included in basic customer service competencies. Libraries receive customers who need resources, and access to those resources should not be blocked by attitudes or negative behavior on the part of staff or leadership. Leaders who communicate acceptance and inclusion demonstrate trust, and as we know, trust creates a culture of service.

When leadership provides a trusting environment but is still faced with a staff member who regularly voices displeasure in working with the public, that person may be in the wrong job. Negative or no-focused customer service may not always result in blatant rudeness, but gestures and tones can also communicate unwillingness to help. Not looking up when a customer approaches the desk to ask a question, a terse look and loud sigh, or folded arms send a message of warning: "Approach with caution—or not at all." Negative body language blocks access to library resources and shuts out the public. If a culture of service groundwork has been laid, but a staff member fails to provide good internal and external customer service, that person's actions must be addressed through coaching, training, or progressive discipline. Staff and leaders who enjoy providing excellent customer service, however, will likely bring positivity into the workplace. Finally, evaluate staff on the ways in which they deliver positive customer service. If staff receive positive customer comments, leaders should acknowledge their efforts and share the information when goals or evaluative discussions are held.

Attitude and Commitment

Staff can be trained in library skills, but trying to develop a positive attitude may be wasted effort. In addition to providing support for staff to make independent decisions in favor of the customer, it's important to hire yes-focused people. Hiring the right people consists of selecting a wide range of thinkers with expertise in a variety of subjects and backgrounds. In addition to looking for any educational or professional degree requirements, leaders should be open to candidates from nonlibrary backgrounds. Food service or customer service experience of any kind indicates that a person already possesses the skills libraries seek: patience, discernment, empathy, and courteousness. Regardless of work experience, interviewees should be able to share concrete examples of how they effectively communicated with customers and how they listened and worked diligently to solve their concerns. Job candidates should behave courteously before, during, and after the interview, and should share enthusiasm for communicating with people. Nordstrom prefers to "hire for the smile and train for skill,"[14] suggesting, "You can teach new people the nuts and bolts, the mechanics of the job, the technical aspects, but you can't teach them to be nice."[15] Pro-customer and pro-team traits are innate tendencies that cannot be taught. Micah Solomon describes why it's important to hire the right people attitudinally and train them technologically and describes traits to look for in "customer-facing"[16] employees: "Warmth: Simple human kindness; Empathy: The ability to sense what another person is feeling; Teamwork: The bias against 'I can do it all myself' and toward 'Let's work together to make this happen'; Conscientiousness: Detail orientation, including an ability and willingness to follow through to completion; and Optimism: The ability to bounce back and not internalize challenges."[17] The traits Solomon describes identify how everyone would like to be treated during transactions: with kindness and empathy. In hiring the best, seek people who find strength in teams rather than self-focused accomplishment, and those who remain optimistic and focused on results to get the job done.

More Than a Paycheck

Once a year, Amazon offers its fulfillment center associates up to $5,000 to quit. Amazon leaders expect that there will be few takers, but do, however, want to offer staff the opportunity to pursue the type of career they want.[18] That's an amazing commitment to ensuring customer service remains stellar. If Amazon employees can be lured away by $5,000, they are not looking to build a career, and further, do not embrace the company philosophy, which is often more valuable than wages. What a brilliant way to keep the best employees, although if the work environment brings happiness and fulfillment, very few staff would take the money.

Similarly, Herb Kelleher, Southwest Airlines CEO, in addressing job satisfaction versus wages, said, "We've never thought that compensation was the primary motivator. If somebody was working just to be compensated, we probably didn't want them at Southwest Airlines."[19] Steve Jobs spent a lot of time recruiting and hiring for Apple; he participated in the hiring of around five thousand people. He based his decisions on his gut and on what a person is like when challenged; Jobs asked the question at every interview, "Why are you here?"[20] Is leadership asking that question of potential new library staff? Questions should be aimed at learning if the potential employee is focused on helping people, and in light of the library's mission and goals, making sure the person in the interview room is up for the challenge.

Arthur Blank and Bernie Marcus are the creators of Home Depot. They started the business after losing their jobs at Handy Dan's Home Improvement Centers in 1978. Blank and Marcus had a goal of building the "first nationwide chain of home improvement stores based on low prices, massive selection, and high customer service."[21] Blank and Marcus always recognized that customer loyalty was at the core of their business model and that customers needed to be treated right. Critical to that connection were the employees, who provided the service that drove the success of Home Depot. Marcus stated in an interview, "Remember most customers are on loan. But if the customer is loyal to you, your company will be good, no matter what else happens."[22] Loyal customers are created by loyal staff who possess an attitude of service modeled by the organization's leadership.

Encouragement

Encouragement is developed by leaders as a result of providing a trusting environment that elicits inclusion and staff buy-in. It's important for leaders to get to know all staff in the library and schedule visits with them regularly. Leaders need to care about staff, including listening to their challenges, concerns, and successes. Encourage staff to get involved in library-wide projects or serve on task teams. Staff will want to contribute to a project that they've been encouraged to take on. Leaders who encourage staff will in turn receive encouragement.

Staff bound by excessive strictness and limited decision making will not be able to respond to customers with personalized service, because they are limited by a fixed number of responses based on rules. *Quick and Nimble* author Adam Bryant suggests, "People throughout organizations often have plenty of ideas. They're on the front lines, seeing how things work, how they don't work, and how they can be made to work better. They hear customers describing problems they love to see solved, and they notice points of friction and inefficiency inside the company. The role of the corporate leader is to create a culture that channels those ideas, that energy, into solutions that matter."[23]

Richard Branson, one of the most remarkable entrepreneurs ever, created Virgin Airlines, a premier customer-oriented airline, without knowing a single thing about the industry except that he was dissatisfied with his own flying experience. While not formally educated in business school, Branson created eight billion-dollar companies in eight different industries—all despite living with the challenges of dyslexia and attention deficit disorder from his youth. There are many factors that contributed to Branson's innovations, but he always acknowledged the people in his businesses for their contribution, to the extent that he did not separate business success from his employees, who made the businesses soar.

A Better Boss

"Project Oxygen" was a mission Google embarked on to "build better bosses."[24] Google used its internal data to learn why employees were unhappy with their bosses and to help bosses learn how to become better. This study revealed that employees leave a company for one or more of three reasons: "The first is that they don't feel a connection to the mission of the company, or sense that their work matters. The second is that they don't really like or respect their co-workers. The third is they have a terrible boss—and this was the biggest variable."[25]

Money, surprisingly, was not a factor in the top three reasons for employees leaving their jobs. Feeling connected to the library mission and sensing that their work matters is empowering and allows staff to have an impact on customer service in monumental ways. Binding staff by restrictive and hierarchical protocols inhibits creativity and detracts from job satisfaction. Equipping staff to manage customer requests independently reinforces their sense of good judgment and connects them to the library mission. What better way to let a staff person know his or her work matters than to trust him or her to decide the best course of action for the customer request. This requires the supervisor, manager, or director to relinquish some control and trust staff to learn from their own mistakes without fear of reprisal. Staff, above all, need hope, support, and encouragement to accomplish positive customer service outcomes.

Support

While it's effective to draw on library models to test or measure a new library-specific product or service, exploring outside the library allows us to see how libraries measure up to the competition. Healthy profits are the proof of business success, and even though library success isn't measured in dollars, business leaders and library leaders aspire to grow their organizations. Library leaders have everything to gain by applying some hard-earned lessons shared by well-known leaders. Leading a successful business or any organization depends on the company culture, and in particular, on how people are treated—whether customers or staff.

Give staff freedom to make mistakes without guilt, invite dumb questions, and praise staff who ask questions that everyone else is afraid to ask. The library's customer service culture development depends on it. The term "culture" describes the fickle environment that drives how people in libraries think, behave, and work. Every library has its own unique environment, in which staff and leadership share their own ways, customs, and beliefs. How library culture is nurtured or ignored determines whether it will thrive or die. The ability to lead a thriving library depends on its leadership, regardless of how phenomenal its products or services are. Whether leading a Fortune 500 company or a governmental agency, great leaders create a culture of trust within their entire organization. The key is creating both a culture of trust and commitment to service. The extent to which that culture is shared with your audience will determine the library's reach in its community.

Staff can handle situations when given the freedom to make decisions and sustain and support leadership during rocky times. A correlation exists between relinquishing control and the development of trust by your staff. Trusting the decisions made by your staff will require you to trust staff more than yourself.[26] Remember for a moment the most effective library leader you ever worked alongside. How would you describe his or her trust in your abilities? Boundaries of hierarchy disappear when you work with great library leaders; they share in accomplishments and defeat and eliminate barriers to free thinking. The best library leaders seldom speak the word "I," but favor the use of "we." Leaders steeped in selfishness don't want to relinquish their power over others, which can stifle staff with fear. Anxiety arises from feelings of loss of control. An example of this in the workplace is when staff feel cut out of the decision-making process—decisions they are expected to implement when working with the public. Leaders must be willing to share their thoughts with the entire library staff, and in doing so release all of their brilliant ideas. Hand over the ideas to others, who can develop them into something better than you ever dreamed. Consider also allowing staff to scrap an idea initiated by leadership. Admit mistakes and share screwups. If you keep ideas hidden for fear that they may be scoffed at, stolen, or not implemented your way, challenge your own thinking by entrusting your idea to a think-partner. This demonstrates your commitment to empower staff and let go of command control.

Staff as Leaders

Frontline library staff demonstrate their leadership every day when they open the library and invite the public to participate in all the wonderful resources the library offers. A robust customer service focus allows leaders to let go of the commanding hierarchy, which should have disappeared in public libraries years ago. Leading a library toward a culture of customer service begins with trust, a shared mission, and clear communication. When staff are given the opportunity to lead in their area of expertise, those in supervisory positions will be called on less often to intervene in customer challenges, which will be solved at the first point of contact. When staff fear making a mistake in providing excellent customer service, it's time to review library structure for elitism and impermeable silos. Silos are generally formed in businesses (or libraries) when work groups don't want to share information among departments. Obviously, silos prevent the sharing of team achievements as well as sharing challenges. Eliminating silos requires library staff working together across the organization, not just working for a supervisor. Adam Bryant's *Quick and Nimble* describes ways to help eliminate silos by regularly holding meetings in person or through videoconferencing and calls, town halls, or any group activities that unite staff and eliminate the void of information.[27] When staff work in an atmosphere absent of information, they will fill in the void with information that leads them to think something has gone awry.[28] By allowing staff to "own" customer problems and solve them with their own good judgment, the customer will be happier, and staff will have more opportunities to personally excel in customer service.

Companies with exceptional customer service rarely go out of business. A strong culture of customer service is imperative to any organization's or business's success, and public library administrators can use such companies as models. Ron Kaufman spent twenty-five years studying the philosophies of company service cultures all over the world and interviewed thousands of team members and leaders. Kaufman noted that although many business leaders were motivated to succeed by the struggle to compete, achieve, merge, penetrate, or conquer, the constant in their success was a "clear architecture for engineering a powerful service culture."[29] Kaufman noted that when organizations' priorities were not focused on a culture of service that was clearly organized by leadership throughout different departments, their businesses struggled and failed to thrive. Kaufman places leaders at the apex of service leadership, which, if effective, permeates every job, role, and situation.[30]

Empowerment, authority, enablement, permission—all power-invoking terms that describe library staff supported by library leadership. Micah Solomon, in "High Tech, High-Touch Customer Service," describes staff empowerment in terms of autonomy and freedom.[31] Solomon makes the case for giving employees flexibility in when and how the job gets done, suggesting that employees will "sprint to any employer offering more freedom."[32] If this is true for employees who work in high-tech industries, could it not also be applied to our library staff who embrace leadership's vision for the library?

Library staff spend the majority of their day assessing the needs of the customer and deciding the best course of action. It can be an exhausting process. Support from leaders will mean everything to those staff who share their vision to exceed customer expectations. Reward staff who embrace the library vision to develop a culture of service. Staff on the front lines need to be supported, particularly after stressful incidents, and it's imperative that you allow staff time to decompress away from the public for a brief time. When challenging interactions take their toll on staff, leadership must show support by encouraging self-care. Because frontline staff are in the center of library activity, support from leadership ensures they can handle any situation that arises.

Inghilleri and Solomon, in "Exceptional Service, Exceptional Profit," describe how new staff orientation can be used to "instill new values, attitudes, and beliefs."[33] Profits aside, library leaders can glean suggestions for training new staff to embrace organizational goals. Psychologists have shown that people are inclined to adopt new roles, goals, and values when they are in disorienting situations, which certainly can be applied to those beginning a new job.[34]

Rather than focusing on the orientation process, give directional and process-related advice, Inghilleri and Solomon suggest, keeping "the focus on what is most crucial for your business: core customer service principals, your company values, and why and how your employee is an essential part of the company's overall mission."[35] Solomon's advice for onboarding? Invite the company CEO to personally deliver information on the organization's values, beliefs, and purpose.[36] Because we know that the first impression made on the new staff will be a lasting one, leaders should invest in the library's culture of service by articulating the vision and inspiration for the library. Encouraging staff to consistently provide service excellence and explaining why it is crucial to the mission of the public library illustrates staff's essential role in implementing the mission, and as a result staff are primed to creatively solve customer needs.

Creating a Yes! Culture, by Anne Cain, Library Director, Retired

Unfortunately there is no one "secret ingredient" that will guarantee a library work unit or team will be engaged, effective, and efficient. Managers and supervisors frequently report having difficulty "making people change." In fact, you cannot make people change, but you can create an environment in which change is the norm or expectation. And there are numerous behaviors, actions, and considerations that managers of high-functioning teams have in common, including the following:

- **Constantly think about yourself in terms of credibility, trust, and integrity.**

  Credibility, trust, and integrity are hard to earn, easy to lose, and doubly hard—possibly impossible—to earn back once they are lost. Always remember that the true test of character is to do the right thing even when no one is looking. Take the high road; do the right thing—even if it is not popular or easy.

- **Set a good example.**

  Lead by example, not "do as I say, not what I do." Model the behaviors you want to see. No matter how many times you tell people to do something, it won't have the same impact as seeing you do it just once. In addition, your willingness to step in shows that you understand and respect the work that is done by your team. The same goes for your attitude: if you are negative some of the time, you cannot expect your staff not to be negative.

- **Trust.**

  Always start from a position of trust with everyone. Assume best intentions—until you have reasons not to trust. I recommend taking a long-range view of all staff. Think of them as if they will be your employees for thirty years (even though most of them will not be there nearly that long). Over the course of a career, all staff are going to have a time when they need some special consideration. Very few of us get through life without having to deal with personal challenges. In addition to working in the library, your staff are also parents to children who need child care, kids struggling in school or who are sick, or wayward teens in need of parental supervision. They may be struggling with financial problems; dealing with their own or a loved one's illnesses or substance abuse problems; working on marital, partnership, or relationship issues; or serving as caregivers to elderly parents. As their manager, you need to learn to recognize the signs that tell you when you can and should help, when someone is abusing the trust you have in him, when kindness and compassion is warranted, and when discipline is called for.

- **Live by the "Golden Rule."**

  The golden rule, as you know, basically says treat others as you would like to be treated, but it comes with a major modification for managers: treat others as you think they would want to be treated. Each person will respond to a different motivation and communication style. It is not about you; it is about them: manage people in the best way for them. In order to do this, managers must develop a broad range of interpersonal and communication skills and styles—and learn what works best with specific individuals and in specific conditions.

- **You will not always be right; take responsibility and expect to make mistakes.**

  When you are wrong, admit it. You are saying that you are wiser today than you were yesterday. One of the best bosses I worked for reminded me many times: "If you are perfect and never make mistakes it means you are not trying hard enough, not taking enough risks." Exceptional managers always acknowledge their mistakes and take ownership. It is not weak, misguided, or wishy-washy to retreat from a position when you realize that someone else's idea might be better. Always take responsibility for things that go wrong. If someone on your team failed to understand a project, if she was not properly trained to handle a situation, or if he misinterpreted a policy, this is on you. It is your responsibility to have an adequately trained staff, and it is your responsibility to ensure that your staff understand instructions, policies, and directions. While this is really hard initially, you will see over time that when staff know that they will not be "blamed" for something going wrong, they will be much more likely to make changes, take risks, be innovative, and cooperate with you—even when they disagree with you.

- **Learn from every challenge and experience.**

  Take a few moments to reflect on why something didn't go well or didn't have the outcome you expected. Think about your approach and thought process—what could you have done differently? There are always new skills to learn and new abilities to master; being able to apply the lessons you learn is one of the best ways to continue to grow.

- **Step out of your comfort zone on a regular basis.**

  Especially for new managers and supervisors, this can be incredibly difficult. If you were the best at children's storytimes and you now manage children's services, it is time to develop the next, new, best storyteller. If you were a great technician or trainer in IT and now manage a group of technical folks, it is time to identify and nurture someone to be even better than you were. The new people coming along will know things you don't know and do many things even better than you did—celebrate this! When this happens, you will know that you have done your job well, as it is your job to bring out the very best in other people!

- **Set a positive tone.**

  Managers set the tone for the work environment. Try to be positive at all times. Look at things in a positive light. Look for opportunities that present themselves while dealing with problems. Do not dwell on obstacles. I always prefer what I call a "no drama" approach. Every work unit provides unlimited potential for distraction: gossip, personal relations (good and bad), office politics, etc. Assume that your staff have enough drama in their personal lives; you don't want to waste time and energy with more drama in the workplace.

- **Strengthen team members.**

  Successful managers match their management approach to each employee's personality and performance level. While in many areas you want to treat people equally, you can and should vary your management style to fit the specific individual. Following are examples of ways to respond to the various personalities of your staff. If someone is

  ○ cautious and orderly, give advance notice of changes and ask for his or her input;

  ○ optimistic, idealistic, and sets schedules and deadlines, encourage thoroughness and give him or her an idea or a cause to promote;

  ○ supportive, comment on his or her effect on morale and make sure he or she interacts with lots of other people; or

  ○ traditional, introduce change slowly and compliment the person on his or her perseverance.

- **Strengthen the team.**

  In addition to helping each individual do her very best, make sure your team functions well and is effective as quickly as possible. I use the word "team" here to refer to both the entire work unit you supervise as well as smaller work groups or task teams you assemble to accomplish a specific purpose. These insights relate to the dynamics of teams of all kinds. Think about each team member's strengths. Look for potentially complementary strengths to offset weaknesses in others.

- **Encourage shared responsibility.**

  It is best to set a tone that communicates that it is everyone's responsibility to keep an eye on things. The manager is ultimately responsible, but by helping everyone feel connected and equally responsible for the team's efforts, you increase the likelihood that there will be good communication and smooth operations among team members. Although managers are expected to attend more meetings, participate in the workings of the larger organization, and maintain external relations and partnerships, it is important to also stay involved in the functions and operations of your work unit. Get in the trenches so that you understand the problems and the customers that your staff are dealing with.

- **Communicate carefully.**

   Be sure you distinguish fact from fiction and that you utilize information that is accurate and complete. Continually evaluate the effectiveness of your communication and, most important, create and maintain a positive climate for the sharing of information.

- **Seek advice and different perspectives.**

   Talk over your ideas with stakeholders, including both older and younger colleagues. Don't present your ideas fully formed—get some consultation. Everyone will want to leave an imprint on a great idea, and this will help ensure successful implementation. Be sure to marry ideas and process. When you want to get something done or have a good idea, the very first question you should ask yourself is about process: Who would be interested, either favorably or unfavorably? Who would it impact? Will it make more work for another department? Always err on the side of inclusiveness.

- **See resistance as feedback.**

   Never complain that your staff are unwilling to change; look for deeper meaning. In fact, the number of people who really don't like change is very small. When resistant, staff may be expressing their concern about their ability to be successful with the proposed changes. You want your staff to be successful, and if you view resistance as feedback, you will start to understand what you can do to create an environment that welcomes change. For example, can you investigate phased implementation of changes? Can you offer additional training? Can you increase staff involvement in planning and implementation? Take into consideration cultural diversity as well as diversity in learning and personality styles.

- **Motivate your staff.**

   What is the best way to motivate people? Studies consistently find that employees are not solely or even truly motivated by money, which is a good thing for library managers, because providing additional money is probably not within your power. Instead, give recognition and acknowledge accomplishments in meaningful, appropriate ways. Use recognition as a powerful tool for building strong working relationships and for motivating others. Find opportunities to call attention to the work of those in your group. Individuals in your work group have different motivations; know what they would want. Do they want to serve on a library-wide committee? Do they want to learn about the operation of another department? Someone seeking a better work/life balance might be motivated by telecommuting days or flexible hours. Others will be motivated by factors such as achievement, extra responsibility, praise, or a sense of camaraderie. Look outside the library for opportunities, too; are there community events, associations, or organizations that would benefit from the talents of your staff?

- **Make time for your team.**

  When you are a manager or leader, it is easy to get so wrapped up in your own workload that you don't make yourself available to your team. Once you're in a management role, your team should always come first. Yes, you have projects that you need to deliver, but your people must come first. Without you being available when they need you, they will not have the support and guidance that they need to meet their objectives.

- **Find the balance between "hands-off" and "hands-on" management.**

  This is also known as "laissez-faire" vs. "micromanagement," and it's another area in which managers walk a fine line. You want to make every project, every output, the best that the team can produce—not the work of an individual. Give credit where credit is due, but first make it the best that it can be with significant input. Most managers want to avoid micromanagement, but going to the opposite extreme (with a hand-offs management style) isn't a good idea, either. You need to find the right balance for your own situation. You really want to avoid having someone on your team complete an important, time-consuming project, only to find that he or she misunderstood the project's scope or specifications because you did not stay in touch. Take responsibility; this is on you.

- **Encourage your staff to be flexible and to look for a way to say "yes" when interpreting policies.**

  If their default position is to say "no," then they (and you) are headed for rocky times. Encourage staff to think about why a policy was enacted in the first place and to consider whether the situation is the same now. Always emphasize using common sense and good judgment. Policies created to ensure a safe environment should probably always be enforced, whereas there might be circumstances in which flexibility can be used with policies that were created to regulate the use of scarce resources. Examples might include making exceptions when collecting fines or extending the time allowed for using a computer or a study room at less busy times.

- **Provide leadership opportunities and focus on developing talent.**

  Be known as someone who cares about staff growth and development and give your team members opportunities to lead within the team. Even something small, like rotating the chairing of meetings, is important. You will see a direct link between talent development and team performance. Finding great new team members and developing the skills needed for your team's success can be some of the more fun responsibilities of a manager or supervisor. There are many types of learning and development opportunities that leaders can offer. Provide a solid orientation to the organization, creating a buddy system so that each employee has someone who can learn with him or her and support his or her learning, direct on-the-job training, specific skills training, continuous professional development, an active employee improvement program, and mentoring.

- **Develop "stretch goals."**

  While members of your team are performing and participating at different levels, it is important to work with all of them to develop "stretch goals": goals that will take them just beyond their comfort zone. Challenge them to try something new or different and to acquire new skills and experience. Be sure to clarify what is an acceptable failure. By incorporating stretch assignments, employees can seek out challenges without feeling that mistakes will set them back in their careers or jeopardize their jobs. It may take a lot of your time to help your staff achieve their stretch goals, but it will empower your team members and encourage them to continually set new goals for themselves. Keep in mind that one person's stretch goal may be something that others have mastered. Don't set a goal that is truly impossible; this will just demotivate the team member.

- **Provide lots of opportunities for your staff to "shine."**

  Create or encourage opportunities for your staff to shine. For example, identify someone to research an emerging technology or a new trend in your field and give a presentation to your team or larger organization. Or find opportunities for your staff to give presentations about the library to governing boards, professional associations, regional networks, etc. Help them prepare by reviewing the presentation with them or by providing an opportunity to deliver a trial run of the presentation to other staff before presenting it to a larger or more public audience.

- **Build support for your team.**

  Develop good relationships with peer supervisors and managers. Determine what you can do to help them be successful or how the two units can work together to accomplish a goal of the larger organization. Ask for their and their staff's expertise in managing your team. Offer your team's assistance to others when possible, deferring your own goals or priorities in favor of goals or priorities deemed more pressing by someone above you. Ask to work on a cross-functional team that will provide you with new challenges and more visibility. Offer to add someone from your staff to a larger library or community project. Keep your boss apprised of problems or issues in your unit. You do not want your boss hearing about things from someone else.

- **Collaborate on decisions and encourage participative management.**

  In the workplace, the most effective decisions tend to be "collaborative." Shared decision making usually results in the best decisions and the easiest implementation. Work with your team to make decisions that are based on community needs and priorities. Encouraging team member participation is one of the most important aspects of effective decision making. The benefits of including team member participation include higher employee motivation, self-confidence, and self-esteem; increased creativity and initiative; and more accountability and productivity.

- **Problem solve.**

  Good solutions to problems emerge when your team members cooperate with one another. Exceptional managers spend time helping the team resolve conflicts and reach consensus. Conflict in and of itself is neither good nor bad. Organizations that avoid conflict avoid change. When there is no conflict, nothing changes. Conflict represents an opportunity to reconsider, which can lead to breakthrough thinking. Libraries that approach conflict in positive and productive ways can provide customers with new and innovative solutions. Conflict is natural and is to be expected, even encouraged, when you have a diverse group with different backgrounds, expectations, personalities, points of view, and work habits. In your work group you will clearly see conflict arising from personalities, behaviors, situations, actions, assignments, and communication. Your goal is not to avoid conflict; rather, you need to learn to manage it effectively so that it leads to organizational improvement—not dysfunction. How you lead your team in times of conflict determines whether you have "good" or "bad" conflict.

- **Speak with passion!**

  Since others may not think of libraries and the work we do as essential (unlike public safety, health and human services, etc.), I always emphasize the essential role libraries play and frame my thoughts and arguments with my passion for what we do. I value and use data, but I also talk about **early literacy** (rather than story hours or children's programs), how libraries foster **civic engagement** (rather than library programming), how we **support students** and narrow or close the achievement gap, how libraries **foster STEM and STEAM learning**, that we provide a **space and options for at-risk youth**, are the place to go for **lifelong learning**—and, most important, **how we make a difference**. How does your library make a difference to your community, students, faculty, etc.? Be prepared to communicate your passion.

- **Watch trends.**

  To sustain and evolve your library's culture of learning, you and your staff need to stay on top of trends and emerging issues, considering how to apply them locally. In addition to keeping up with what's happening in libraries, it is also important for you to keep up to date with nonlibrary trends.

Remember that you are not a leader unless you engage followers!

Yes! on Demand starts with leaders dedicated to creating a culture of customer service. Library leadership must acknowledge and empower employees so they can fully exercise their heroic "powers" on the front line. Super-powered staff fueled on yes-focused service can save the day when they receive support, encouragement, and trust from library leaders. Staff are the library's most important resource in public libraries today, and they are essential to personalizing each person's library experience; most of all, they are the heroes on the front line of library service.

NOTES

1. Dave Gray and Thomas Vander Wal, *The Connected Company* (Sebastopol, CA: O'Reilly, 2012), 255.

2. Richard Branson, *The Virgin Way: Everything I Know about Leadership* (New York: Penguin Group, 2014), 215.

3. Ibid., 120.

4. Ibid.

5. John A. Byrne, *World Changers* (New York: Penguin Group, 2011), 179.

6. Robert Spector and Patrick McCarthy, *The Nordstrom Way* (Hoboken, NJ: John Wiley & Sons, 2005), 113.

7. Simon Sinek, *Leaders Eat Last* (New York: Penguin Group, 2014), 29.

8. Ibid.

9. Ibid.

10. Ibid., 29.

11. Ibid., 30.

12. Ibid.

13. Ibid.

14. Spector and McCarthy, *The Nordstrom Way*, 91.

15. Ibid., 106.

16. Micah Solomon, *High-Tech, High-Touch Customer Service* (New York: AMACOM, 2012), 93.

17. Ibid.

18. Amazon, "Working at Amazon," https://www.amazon.com/p/feature/nssax wpeeyzuvah?ref_=aa_navb_5&pf_rd_r=9BS3HAKEE4AANSMMAT3J&pf_rd _p=bb5a904e-8bb9-4ed0-a909-5839bd830411 (accessed December 27, 2015).

19. Byrne, *World Changers*, 76.

20. Ibid., 91.

21. Ibid., 24.

22. Ibid., 35.

23. Adam Bryant, *Quick and Nimble* (New York: Henry Holt, 2014), 188.

24. Adam Bryant, "Google's Quest to Build a Better Boss," *New York Times*, March 12, 2011, http://www.nytimes.com/2011/03/13/business/13hire.html?_r=0.

25. Ibid.

26. Sinek, *Leaders Eat Last*, 143.

27. Bryant, *Quick and Nimble*, 178.

28. Ibid.

29. Ron Kaufman, *Uplifting Service* (New York: Evolve Publishing, 2012), 80.

30. Ibid., 81.

31. Solomon, *High-Tech, High-Touch Customer Service*, 98.

32. Ibid.

33. Leonardo Inghilleri and Micah Solomon, *Exceptional Service, Exceptional Profit* (New York: AMACOM, 2010), 90.

34. Ibid., 90–91.

35. Ibid., 91.

36. Ibid.

3

Yes! on Demand

Personalized service is often associated with concierge service—a service that attends to people who usually have more money than time. A true concierge arranges activities that make the customer's dreams come true by listening to his or her wishes and exceeding the expected. Personalized library service attains the same level of delight as concierge service. It surpasses customer expectations and lures customers back for return visits to repeat the experience. But you may be thinking, "Personalized service is too time consuming" or "You don't know the challenges I'm faced with every day" or "We don't have enough staff to offer concierge service." When it's made a priority, personalized customer service is much easier to provide than standard customer service. Personalized customer service results in happy customers and happy staff; happy customers embrace the library for life.

Successful businesses make it their goal to provide customers with happy experiences. Disneyland, Zappos, and Amazon declare happiness to be part of their mission. Those in public libraries can also leverage happiness through service that brings joy and delight to customers when they discover something new in the library that enhances their lives. The power of happiness cannot be overestimated for its ability to attract and retain library customers. Disneyland created its success on exceeding customer expectations for happiness: "At Disney, we try to create happiness for people of all ages everywhere. This common purpose is our rallying flag. It aligns the efforts of cast members and establishes a foundation for their own behavior toward guests."[1] Disney recognizes that its employees (cast members) are the most important asset and over the past fifty years has reported that employees are the primary reason that guests return.[2] Library staff also hold the key to attracting new, and retaining current, customers.

Steven Bell explores the topic of library happiness and suggests that libraries stand ready to deliver such experiences through simple learning and exploring experiences unique to libraries.[3] "To achieve totality, the same experience—ideally one that is memorable, differentiated, and capable of producing loyalty—is delivered at the threshold of the facility, at the service desk, on the phone, in the stacks, and anywhere else a community member interacts with the library."[4] The memorable experiences that result in customer loyalty can only be delivered by library staff where and when they are able to meet the customer's demand for personalized service. The extent to which staff deliver happy experiences depends on their ability to recognize and act on customer cues that direct the path to happiness.

The way in which leaders create happiness begins with caring, not only about the product and services the business offers, but also about customers and employees. The most respected entrepreneurs in the world genuinely care about both customers and staff, in contrast to profit margins alone. Herb Kelleher, an entrepreneur whom Richard Branson admires and discusses in *The Virgin Way*, places the highest value possible on relationships built with customers. Kelleher was known for creating "one of the most enjoyable places to work in America," at Southwest Airlines.[5] Kelleher's business culture is centered on happiness and connections made in employees' personal lives. In 2011 Southwest received the best customer-satisfaction record of any airline in America, with the fewest complaints filed per 100,000 carried.[6] Tossing aside convention, Southwest manages its human resource department through its People Department, which is indicative of Kelleher's respect for and commitment to staff. "We always felt that if you allow people to be themselves at work, they will enjoy what they are doing. . . . We've always tried to be sensitive to the needs of our people and recognize the things that are important to them in their personal lives."[7] Customer service is bound up in caring about and respecting staff.

A library's mission statement should follow a service concept that the whole organization can believe in and consistently deliver, because service is a shared value that teams work on together. *Yes! on Demand* customer service requires staff empowerment for determining what's best—what will create happiness—for library customers. Staff will find solutions to barriers that block access to library products and services when given permission to do so. Engaged and empowered employees bring delight to the customer experience.

Complaints are simply suggestions in disguise. When viewed as opportunities to learn how to improve service, complaints can reveal barriers that customers find frustrating and impractical. Ask to be given the next escalated customer complaint, to practice your skills. Find the hidden gem buried in the complaint and start out by assuming the customer has a legitimate complaint. Greet the customer with the intention of finding a solution that will bring happiness to his or her day, and listen for cues that might be buried in emotion. Perhaps the customer felt insulted, disrespected, challenged, or simply unheard. After dedicating the time needed to understand the complaint, try responding with, "What will make you happy today?" or "How can I make that right for you?" Questions that point directly at making the customer's day improve both surprise and delight customers. Customers complain because they meet unyielding barriers to something they want. What drives complaints? The people at Apple make a point of calling dissatisfied customers within twenty-four hours, because they want to build a loyal customer base. Apple research has calculated that every hour Apple spends on unhappy customers or "detractors" of business results in an incremental $1,000 of revenue.[8] Applying the same principle to libraries makes sense. Responding quickly to complaints adds library promoters, in contrast to detractors who share their dissatisfaction with others. Dedicating uninterrupted time to listening to customer complaints is essential for solving the customer's problem. Reviewing any outdated or irrelevant library procedures might result in changes a customer complained about. Freedom to achieve customer happiness begins with staff acting in ways that demonstrate "yes."

Unempowered staff often find themselves in the position of defending library policy and procedures regardless of the customer's dilemma. In order to defend the library's viewpoint and their own actions, staff cite policy and procedures. As a result, the transaction deteriorates into an uncaring and impersonal exchange, with the library on top and the customer on the bottom. Whether a transaction revolves around lost books, fines, or suggestions for improving library service, it's important to dig deeper, past the symptoms to the cause for concern. Customer suggestions for improvement should be considered in light of enhancing and expanding services, not to maintain the status quo.

Consider the library customer who e-mails the library director to request drive-up service. That's a big request and on the surface has "no" written all over it. Rather than provide reasons why it cannot be done, or suggesting it be added to a list of possibilities, ask how a drive-up would improve customers' library experiences. As a result of listening to reasons why a drive-up would enhance her life, we learn that the customer struggles with access and doesn't want to give up coming to the library. Accompanied by several small children, all of whom ride in car seats, she says that just getting the kids in and out of car seats while lugging piles of picture books inside can be difficult. As a result of the customer's need, which could be more broadly applied, the library director suggests staff look at ways to implement curbside pick-up and delivery service. Why not? Customers enjoy it and expect restaurants to provide it. It's convenient and an improvement on drive-up service. While the library cannot deliver on drive-up service, it can provide a solution for the customer's need: quick, easy, and convenient access. Curbside service also benefits people with mobility challenges. The idea for curbside service resulted from taking the time to empathize with the customer's need and to figure out how to address it.

Personalizing responses to complaints demonstrates the library's commitment to yes-focused service. A customer's initial complaint does not usually reflect its root cause or motive. For instance, a customer complains about being treated unfairly and intends to sue the library over its service animal regulations. As it turns out, the unruly dog growling at staff and customers is actually a pet. In the end, the only real complaint is the customer's response to being required to remove the pet from the library, not the intent to sue over federal law. It has become common for customers to bring pets into businesses. Customers with dogs browse boutique shops, stroll grocery aisles, and allow their pets to sit beneath tables at outdoor restaurants. Nordstrom provides water for pets who accompany their owners shopping. The pet trend, which is unlawful in public libraries, puts staff in the difficult position of enforcing service animal rule compliance. Library staff are the first to address the pet's visit, and as deliverers of the message, the first to face the fallout. Because only service animals may accompany customers into the library, a customer may become defensive when asked if the animal is a pet or service animal, or when asked what service the animal provides. Because other businesses have allowed or ignored pet visits, library staff are looked upon as being unreasonable and intolerant. Offending a person's pet is akin to offending his or her child.

In one particular instance, an outraged customer called the library to express her dissatisfaction with the way library staff handled her pet-accompanied visit. The customer did not complain about the questions asked by staff but about the manner in which the questions were framed. After talking with her for several minutes, it became clear that she knew her pet was not allowed in the library before she visited. The customer explained that she felt embarrassed and humiliated when staff asked her questions about her pet in front of other people in the library. She felt attacked and singled out. She stewed over her library experience for a few days before reporting it. She explained that it bothered her so much that she couldn't forget it. It bothered her for hours that evening, and she shared her story with family and friends. Finally, she contacted the library to complain. The customer's feelings of embarrassment and humiliation were acknowledged, without judging or guessing at her motives. When reduced further, the complaint stemmed from staff challenging her truthfulness in answering the service animal question. She had initially stated that her animal was a service provider, but it was not. Later she admitted the dog was her pet. Her integrity was publicly challenged, and she reacted defensively.

Yes! on Demand does not mean saying "yes" to every customer and breaking every rule. There are many ways to provide yes-like answers with boundaries. Answers rooted in "yes" allow for positive results and keep the dialogue open and supportive. Validate the customer's feelings, and if rules cannot or should not be bent, let the customer know you are working toward an appropriate solution. In matters of customer behavior, safety, and law, customer interactions should be personalized for the degree of the violation. Asking the parent of an unceasingly crying baby to step outside for a few moments addresses customer behavior expectations, and would be handled differently than asking a person who took a swig of whiskey from his or her front coat pocket to leave the library.

When dealing with sensitive behavior concerns, start the conversation by first greeting the customer in a positive way. "Hello, how are you doing today? I see you have your dog with you today—is this your service animal?" If the response is "No," you can continue with: "You probably didn't know this, but pets aren't allowed in the library. Would it be possible for you to return to the library later without your pet?" When possible, engage customers in a conversation based in solutions for their access to library resources. If you are met with resistance, move toward a firm but polite request to leave the library. If increased resistance is met, reiterate the need to exit and give the customer time and space in which to do so. When transactions are conducted with kindness and empathy, most customers comply. However, if you are met with hostility or verbal abuse, end the conversation and follow up with protocol to remove the customer, with a call to either law enforcement or security. No harm will result if the patron remains in the library with the pet while you make a phone call or summon additional help. It's not a battle of wills that's needed, it's patience. The customer will often leave after law enforcement is called.

Start difficult conversations by greeting the customer in order to get the discussion off to a good start and to make a personal connection: offer a yes-focused solution (customer can stay, dog must go); empathize with the customer's situation (being asked to leave is inconvenient, unplanned, and causes embarrassment); reiterate the request and provide space for compliance; and follow library guidelines for removing customers with challenging behavior. In addition to the face-to-face or telephone complaints staff receive, customers are voicing their concerns for the entire world to review on the Web.

SOCIAL NETWORKS

Social networks have changed the way in which customers share complaints, and they are weighing in online to slam public libraries and staff. Networked customers also find advice and answers quickly and easily through other customers' experiences. Libraries are quickly losing their long-held position as arbiters of knowledge. People want fast, easy recommendations for reading, library parking, access, service, cleanliness, safety, rules, and policies. Customers read comments to learn whether the library is worth visiting or not. Gray and Vander Wal, in *The Connected Company*, suggest that 90 percent of customers trust recommendations from other customers more than any other type of advertising.[9] Networking provides customers with a means to connect globally in a way that can be powerfully helpful or detrimental at the same time. Trolling your library's Yelp comments provides a starting place for assembling your customers' experiences into actionable improvements.

Perhaps the concept of providing personalized customer service seems daunting in light of competing off-desk responsibilities and workloads. Any service delivered on the front lines, and specifically personalized customer service, requires a positive culture and the support of library leadership. With the backing of library leadership, staff are free to make decisions that develop customer happiness and loyalty. Providing *Yes! on Demand* service face-to-face or via chat or e-mail requires only a few impactful moments, but it will make a lasting difference in the customer's life. Personalized service begins with all library employees communicating a receptive attitude and the ability to listen for clues that lead to the customer's need. Traditional customer service training is inadequate in light of today's savvy customer, who is accustomed to excellent products, quick and efficient transactions, and staff friendliness. Customers enjoy working with staff open to creative ways of problem solving, and likewise staff find freedom in deciding the best course of action.

The largest successful businesses all provide personalized service; their employees are empowered to respond to customer cues that expand the transaction into amazing. Amazon, Zappos, Starbucks, and Apple have risen to the top by delivering products and yes-focused customer service on demand. Doing business with these giants feels personal because the customer service representatives listen closely to requests and provide the product or service that makes the customer happy. Customer service is the top priority, which is obvious to the buyers shopping there. In addition to finding the products they seek, customers know they will enjoy a stress-free experience while shopping.

Most customers who visit Starbucks expect to receive a consistent product, along with friendly, efficient service. Are customers criticized for ordering a venti triple low-fat soy latte with real whipped cream? Of course not. Starbucks not only prepares the drink but also suggests new drinks on days the customer is undecided. If the customer is unsatisfied with the drink, the barista will try again. Customers receive the "unhappy guest" card for a free drink when staff feel they've made customers wait too long or ruined the coffee experience in another way. Greeting customers, Starbucks baristas remember names, use good manners, and engage customers in friendly conversation when appropriate. Customers pay top price for drinks and service, and Starbucks will continue to grow if its products and services center on customer-personalized demand. Customers know what to expect from Starbucks and enjoy a welcoming environment. Some customers read, meet for business, socialize, or just relax. Customers return to Starbucks for its dedication to serving happiness as well as products. Because of Starbucks's dedication to customer service, it's rare to encounter a rude employee there, and unlikely that staff would ever respond with, "We can't make that drink" or "You can't do that here" or "No, no—no!" Starbucks welcomes customers, provides customized drinks, and employs people who are knowledgeable about the products and services it provides.

Starbucks management shares with staff how to personalize relationships with customers in a little pamphlet known as the "Green Apron Book."[10] The culture of customer service created by Starbucks happens not by accident but by intent. Feeling special, noticed, recognized for uniqueness, such as remembering a customer's signature drink order, makes Starbucks customers feel important and welcome. Libraries can adopt this practice by warmly greeting people, remembering their names, and responding to their needs with customized solutions.

Practicing *Yes! on Demand* service requires listening to customers and acknowledging that their needs matter. Just as Starbucks makes a difference in a customer's life by providing a free surprise drink for a person having a terrible day, library staff can also find ways to surprise and delight customers. Consider opening the front doors of the library a few minutes early and announcing, "We're ready to open a little early today. Come in and welcome."

Starbucks leadership encourages staff to connect with customers in a personal way. "True leaders, in other words, show staff that their individual uniqueness gives them a special way to connect with others."[11] Allowing staff to exercise uniqueness leads to a deeper level of service, the type of service that begins with caring about people. Not surprisingly, Starbucks staff are trained to take action immediately to solve customer requests. If a drink isn't prepared to the customer's satisfaction, staff are encouraged to keep trying until the drink fits the customer's taste. If a customer spills a drink before enjoying it, it's replaced. Starbucks staff are empowered to make things right for the customer.[12] What can libraries learn from Starbucks's ways of discovering people's unique needs?

What makes your personal shopping or dining experiences memorable? What makes you want to return for more, or run away? Pleasant or horrible experiences can always be traced back to a person who acted outside the bounds of routine customer service. Going out of bounds in a positive or negative way solidifies the experience and determines customer loyalty or disloyalty. Customer loyalty is bound to customer service—how the employee made the shopper or visitor feel.

Zappos Surprise by Jade S.

I've been a customer of Zappos for a while, so it was a no-brainer for me to shop their Web site for a pair of shoes that I wanted for my wedding. In search of the perfectly whimsical and comfortable wedding shoes, I had ordered, exchanged, and returned <u>five</u> pairs of different sizes and styles of ballerina slippers—in just a week. Yikes! I was convinced Zappos had labeled me a "problem customer." To be honest, I was a little irritated by the time I placed my sixth and final exchange. I wasn't trying to hide how I felt, either! Unwavering, the friendly Zappos phone rep was knowledgeable and eager to help me. The phone rep (let's call her Sue) shared that she was reading "Delivering Happiness" by Zappos founder Tony Hsieh, which I thought was interesting, as it's on my list of books to read. We chit-chatted a little while she looked up my order number and correct size. She was curious about my order, so I explained to Sue that I wanted to wear and decorate the ballet slippers for my wedding. As it turns out, Sue was planning a wedding, too! We talked a little longer about wedding themes, locations, guests, etc. Sue soon finished the transaction and I went about my day. The very next day my slippers arrived. They were a perfect fit, so I marked "buy wedding shoes" off my wedding to-do list.

About a week later an unexpected package arrived at my doorstep. Inside was a beautiful bouquet of fresh flowers and a small note thanking me for my order and congratulating me on my marriage. The flowers and note were sent via Zappos from Sue. Wow! I was surprised to receive a gift from a retail store (of all places), but that gesture left an impression on me. It put a smile on my face and separated Zappos from the rest.

Jade's Zappos story demonstrates several points. The customer service representative recognized that the customer's shoes were an important part of the wedding, while she empathized with the stress brought on by wedding plans. She listened to the customer on a personal level by sharing her own thoughts on wedding plans. The customer's expectations were surpassed. Empowered to provide customer happiness, the employee embraced Zappos's challenge to "wow" the customer through awesome service beyond customer satisfaction.

Zappos mission "to live and deliver WOW" originates from its core values engrained in the company culture: (1) deliver WOW through service; (2) embrace and drive change; (3) create fun and a little weirdness; (4) be adventurous, creative, and open-minded; (5) pursue growth and learning; (6) build open and honest relationships with communication; (7) build a positive and family spirit; (8) do more with less; (9) be passionate and determined; and (10) be humble.[13] Top businesses focus on surpassing customer expectations and making a lasting impression on the customer. Libraries can do the same. Successful businesses are surprising customers with outstanding service because it pays off in profits.

Similar to "Wow" customer service delivered by Zappos, the chief customer officer at MSA–The Safety Company created a "virtual wallet" for its employees to personalize customer service.[14] For example, employees "can use their virtual wallet to drop a freight charge, or accelerate shipping time, or provide additional samples."[15] The virtual wallet allows staff to meet customer demand, which increases company productivity and growth. It allows flexibility for customers and frees staff from restrictive rules that block access. MSA chief customer service officer Gavan Duff argues that the "virtual wallet" creates efficiency and effectiveness for the frontline staff and boosts their morale, which makes doing business for the customer easier.[16]

What resources can libraries provide for customers that invite a "Wow" customer experience and ensure customer loyalty? Libraries are facing the fiercest competition imaginable. The key to sustaining library relevance for the community is based on the library's capacity to compete with competitive products and services delivered in a surprisingly personal way. Empower library staff with a virtual wallet? Sounds like a fun way to deliver happiness.

WHAT *YES! ON DEMAND* ISN'T

Library staff may share concern about how to balance workload with personalized customer service. And as much as they'd like to see challenges in providing personalized service, when staffing is at low levels and lines are building up, serving customers should be the top priority for staff. When the service desk requires more help than one person can provide, library leaders can support staff by scheduling back-up help. If the customer's need is taking second place to any other backroom processes, it's time to redirect the focus where it belongs—to the customer's needs. Suggesting to customers that they return on another day only delays the customer's need and is the antithesis of *Yes! on Demand* service. Arrange for staff from other areas of the library to assist when called.

Backroom processes do not take priority over a customer's need, and with leadership's full support for yes-focused customer service, staff can place the highest priority on meeting customer demands when asked. By empowering staff to personalize transactions even at busy times, leaders can show support by creating schedules that allow for flexible duties during public open hours. Leadership should be willing to model yes-focused service at busy times and when staff need encouragement. Achieving a yes-focused library culture results when all staff work together to address immediate needs voiced by the customer and recognize that customers are the reason public libraries exist. *Yes! on Demand* service requires a commitment from leadership and staff to place the needs of the customer above all other work assignments. No other work processes or off-desk assignments are more important than the customers' requests. Too often, priorities are placed on tasks and not people. *Yes! on Demand* requires more than one person. It requires that everyone, from leadership to the front line, be committed to serving the customer. Schedule staff time to pop out to the information desk for on-demand customer requests, while scheduling nondesk staff to focus on backroom processes. Prioritize program or other types of planning for nonpublic hours, so backup staff can be called out to the desk. Serving customers in person should be the library's highest priority.

In the planning stages and early days of operation of Disneyland, Walt Disney talked with visitors. He observed how people used the park and engaged with visitors to improve the overall customer experience. Walt Disney also required his management team to eat lunch at the park and to listen to what customers were saying as they stood in restaurant lines. That's engagement—that's prioritizing the customer above all else! Because a yes-focused service culture depends on valuing staff as the library's greatest asset and places customers in the apex of service—even when work processes compete for attention—action plans should reflect the new culture. Library customers can inform improvements in library service when staff listen and share what they learn. As valued partners, engaged customers will support the library by sharing ideas.

Businesses placing a strong emphasis on customer service grow in the competitive marketplace, while those without such an emphasis cease to exist. Ron Kaufman, in *Uplifting Service*, suggests that a culture of customer service must first be created in order for a business to succeed.[17] Businesses that fail neglect to acknowledge the power of customer service to sustain and increase customer satisfaction. "There is an amazing constant among the successful companies and organizations I have encountered. A clear architecture for engineering a powerful service emerges over and over again."[18] Successful businesses cannot waste time fighting against customer-focused service by explaining to customers why they cannot provide results. Likewise, public libraries must embrace a similar ethos that places the highest emphasis on customer needs and requests. Breaking down the steps that businesses use to provide *Yes! on Demand* service provides a model for libraries. For example, using profit as the indicator for success, Inghilleri and Solomon, in *Exceptional Service, Exceptional Profit*, suggest that language should make customers feel at ease, not intimidate them.[19] No one wants to do business with a company that raises customer anxiety and stress levels. For instance, "You owe . . ." versus "Our records show a balance of . . ." illustrates the difference between good and bad language choices.[20] For those who work in libraries, it's important to acknowledge that some customers may already feel out of place, may not have visited a library in years, or may be embarrassed to ask a question based on the belief that librarians may be smarter than they are. Good language choice determines the degree to which customers connect with library products and services that affect their lives.

YES AND NO LANGUAGE

No: *You owe . . .*

Yes: *Our records show there's a balance on your account that you might not be aware of.*

No: *Your account is blocked.*

Yes: *I'm looking at your account and want to share with you what I'm seeing. It shows that several items are lost, and I want to make sure you'll get the materials you came in for today.*

No: *We don't have that.*

Yes: *I can have that book delivered to the library for you, or we can search for another title that you might like.*

No: *You can't bring that oversized cart in the library.*

Yes: *Hello, how are you doing today? I'm sorry, we won't be able to accommodate your belongings in the library, but we certainly welcome you to be here.*

A barista at Starbucks recalled a story about a customer who arrived daily for coffee, always in a hurry and barely speaking to staff. The staff continued trying, without success, to personally connect with the customer. The barista recalled that to the surprise of Starbucks staff: "One evening she came in and mentioned that her husband was in the car. Then she thanked us for always delivering the drink in such a nice way and said that though she personally never drank Starbucks, it was the only thing her husband could stomach after his chemotherapy."[21] Staff learned that the customer was preoccupied with her husband's illness, which is why she didn't engage with staff and why she so quickly came and left.

Likewise, library staff may never know what impact they have on a customer's life, unless it's shared with others. One customer wanted to "share his love for the library" by donating a stack of $20.00 bills directly into a library director's hands. This nicely dressed visitor had visited the library several months before when he was experiencing homelessness, and library staff took a few moments to listen to his needs and connect him with resources that resulted in his getting a warm coat in the winter. He'd returned to the library to express his thanks to the staff for their help during a rough time in his life. Staff may never know the impact the library has on people struggling to overcome difficulties.

Getting to "yes" begins with knowing library products and services. In addition to the knowledge, skills, and abilities needed to provide customers with the most appropriate resources, staff must listen empathetically and build trust. Customers enjoy interacting with staff who listen to complaints and suggestions, and are good listeners who can pick up cues to deliver personalized service.

Welcoming customers proves we want them in the library. A simple nod, smile, or hello suggests that customers are friends, not enemies. When library doors open and customers pour in, what kinds of reactions do staff offer, and in what ways do staff welcome customers inside? A simple way to welcome customers begins with facing toward, not away from, them. Turning chairs to face customers or standing in a way that demonstrates that staff are eager to help starts transactions off in the right direction.

Lead customers to the resources or services they need, rather than describing and pointing. Libraries are the Home Depot of books: so many aisles, floors, and confusing stacks to wade through. It takes weeks for new library staff to find everything, so it's easy to imagine customers will appreciate personalized guidance. Home Depot staff walk customers to large ticket items as well as little things, like nuts and bolts. Walking the customer to the source also provides opportunities to learn why the customer chose to use the library and how staff can better serve. Giving service by walking with customers provides extra opportunities to connect in an informal way and eliminates physical barriers that impede conversation. Leading customers to what they need demonstrates that staff care about them and are eager to help. Creating a culture of "yes" also brings work groups together in a common goal and illustrates to stakeholders that staff are involved in making the library a welcome place.

Unspoken cues are essential for providing a welcoming environment for people who speak languages other than English. As Michael Buono discusses in "Risk Looking Stupid," it is uncommon for members of minority groups who don't speak English to receive good customer service, because communication is difficult, even for the most experienced librarians.[22] Speaking in snippets of the customer's language, using apps or pictures, or making gestures can be exhausting for library staff. But there are ways to mitigate the tension and let customers know your intent to understand the request. Buono describes the personal connection that occurs when the language barrier is broken—when a connection is made with the person from a different culture, age group, or minority group: "In that instant, there is a connection. A moment where the language barrier is forgotten, and we are two people figuring out something together. The process can be draining, but the moment you succeed at forming that connection is a sweet thing."[23] Connecting with any library customer can be a sweet thing when staff are empowered to serve the customer in the ways they'd like to be served. Personalizing service requires flexibility and firmness, empathy and steadfastness, and a commitment to offer a balanced and fresh approach with each new customer experience.

NOTES

1. Disney Institute and Theodore B. Kinni, *Be Our Guest* (New York: Disney Editions, 2011), 20.

2. Ibid., 21.

3. Steven Bell, "Life, Library, and the Pursuit of Happiness," *Library Journal*, October7, 2015, http://lj.libraryjournal.com/2015/10/managing-libraries/life-library-and-the-pursuit-of-happiness/#_.

4. Ibid.

5. John A. Byrne, *World Changers* (New York: Penguin Group, 2011), 74.

6. Ibid., 78.

7. Ibid., 75.

8. Dave Gray and Thomas Vander Wal, *The Connected Company* (Sebastopol, CA: O'Reilly, 2012), 107.

9. Ibid., 9.

10. Joseph A. Michelli, *The Starbucks Experience* (New York: McGraw-Hill, 2007), 21.

11. Ibid., 28.

12. Ibid., 15.

13. Tony Hsieh, *Delivering Happiness* (New York: Business Plus, 2010), 159.

14. Jeanne Bliss, *Chief Customer Officer 2.0* (Hoboken, NJ: John Wiley & Sons, 2015), 51.

15. Ibid., 51.

16. Ibid., 52.

17. Ron Kaufman, *Uplifting Service* (New York: Evolve Publishing, 2012), 80–81.

18. Ibid., 81.

19. Leonardo Inghilleri and Micah Solomon, *Exceptional Service, Exceptional Profit* (New York: AMACOM, 2010), 8.

20. Ibid., 16.

21. Michelli, *The Starbucks Experience*, 75–76.

22. Michael Buono, "Risk Looking Stupid," in *Library Services for Multicultural Patrons*, ed. Carol Smallwood and Kim Becnel (Lanham, MD: Scarecrow Press, 2013), 303.

23. Ibid.

4

Business *Yes!* Models

Retailers provide the perfect model for public library customer service. They're experts in *Yes! on Demand*. It's difficult to imagine public library staff as salespeople without the obvious—sales.[1] No funds are exchanged for products or services at the public library, but customer expectations remain the same: customers want access to products and services delivered easily and efficiently by knowledgeable, friendly people. If libraries expect to attract new customers and retain current ones, we must give customers what they want. Consumers will shop for books, digital material, or other community resources outside of the public library when the effort to get what they want outweighs the benefit. They will shop for products and services outside of the public library, and many do so regardless of the price tag. Consumers will pay for easy, convenient service to get what they want, when they want it. Exceptional customer service sets high revenue businesses apart from mediocre businesses. Personalized customer service is essential to ensure the future of the public library.

The businesses discussed below spend millions of dollars on branding, merchandising, inventory, product knowledge, and delivery. They invest heavily in creating a culture that incubates employee loyalty in order to increase profits and thus ensure the future of the company. Employee loyalty grows from a culture of trust and empowerment, and employee selection is based on outrageously friendly customer service skills. Employees of these winning companies are taught to exceed customer expectations, which requires employees to frequently provide service that goes out of bounds. Top profit-making businesses empower the staff they hire to make the customer happy, regardless of whether or not they make the sale, because businesses know that happy customers are loyal customers. This concept is embraced by many top businesses that study consumer behaviors and purchasing trends. Because the focus is placed where it should be, these businesses develop loyal customers who enjoy a positive experience in the hands of capable, dedicated people. Because the service these businesses provide is based on profit, comparing Zappos, for example, with the public library may seem misaligned, but the only differences between the two giants are their funding sources, missions, and profits.

This chapter describes consumer expectations for customer service and examples of how businesses sustain customer loyalty over the years, in contrast to businesses that lose the retail battle due to inconvenient, cumbersome, and outdated services. Apple, Amazon, Disneyland, and others who provide premier customer experiences are contrasted with businesses that have a reputation for missing the mark.

SERVICE INDUSTRY

Neiman Marcus

Customers who can afford to shop at Neiman Marcus know they will be served with a custom buying experience. While Walmart gains huge profits from amassing sales, high-end retailers like Neiman Marcus will sell fewer goods and still earn higher profits. They provide a buying *experience* in contrast to simply selling, and present exclusive designs to customers looking to enhance their self-image. On the scale of service and quality, do public libraries compare with Walmart or Neiman Marcus? Both businesses earn high profits; Neiman Marcus, with fewer sales but higher prices, offers products to a niche clientele, and Walmart offers low prices on products that appeal to the masses.

Neiman Marcus's customer service statement provides a scalable model for application to libraries when products for sale are replaced with products borrowed. Neiman Marcus Group lists as its goal to excel in merchandising, customer service, and marketing. It endeavors to be the best retailer of luxury and fashion and is not content with resting on its past achievements; the company publicizes the fact that it will adapt to its customers' preferences with innovation and engagement in order for customers to shop conveniently anytime and anywhere. Not only is the Neiman Marcus Group the place to find fashion and luxury but it is also where customers will enjoy extraordinary service.[2] In addition to selling Gucci, Prada, and Chanel, Neiman Marcus lures customers in who expect premier customer service. Neiman Marcus encourages and expects its sales associates to make personal connections and lasting relationships with customers. This aspect of Neiman Marcus customer services sets it apart from other retail establishments.[3]

Revenues for major luxury retailers depend on customer service excellence delivered by friendly, knowledgeable employees. In contrast, public libraries do not make or rely on sales to survive. However, the library does rely on votes to pass bonds and tax measures, an equally important consideration for library sustainability. How would Neiman Marcus customer service compare to public library service? Do libraries look for the same qualities that Neiman Marcus does when hiring? The customer-employee connection is essential to the success of Neiman Marcus; the company bases its business on niche customer service. If the customer service standards created for the Neiman Marcus customer were adopted in public libraries, visitors would be completely amazed and delighted. Customers enjoy talking with friendly staff who are interested in learning more about their lives.

Nordstrom

Nordstrom provides customers with a premier custom experience and trains employees to solve problems creatively. Personalized service creates an environment in which staff can make judgment calls in negotiating customer happiness. At Nordstrom, the entire new employee handbook fits on two sides of a card. Nordstrom wants its employees to focus on customer happiness, not policy and procedure. Side one of the card provides a simple, "Welcome to Nordstrom. We're glad to have you with our Company. Our number one goal is to provide outstanding customer service."[4] Side two states: "Our only rule: Use good judgment in all situations."[5] With these amazingly simple precepts, Nordstrom stands behind its employees to do whatever it takes to make the customer happy. Empowered staff are the key to Nordstrom's sales, and employee efforts to create happiness are regularly celebrated. When an employee goes above and beyond in customer service, fellow employees submit their observations to management. Stories that reach the highest level are posted to a customer service All-Star board in the store where the employee works.[6] Public acknowledgment honors and rewards the employee for exceptional service, but this also broadcasts to all employees that Nordstrom leadership places a high emphasis on achieving over-the-top customer service. Nordstrom recognizes that staff are key to growing sales, whether they help customers in person or online.

Nordstrom's 2015 SWOT (strengths, weaknesses, opportunities, and threats) analysis acknowledges that customer loyalty is becoming more difficult to achieve, and the company has undergone tremendous changes in the past few years. The report bears significance for the changing demands of customers in general and could easily be describing today's public library. Nordstrom acknowledges that customers are changing, and so must the company. Because customers have less time and are more technologically knowledgeable than in the past, they expect more from their shopping experiences at their favorite retailers. Customers expect to shop their way and are savvy in multiple ways to do so.[7] The report also addresses weaknesses in Nordstrom by acknowledging the choices consumers have due to Internet and mobile commerce. Like Nordstrom customers, library customers have also become pressed for time and have become more technically savvy and demanding; many are no longer satisfied waiting for what they want. Library customers will run to retailers who are ready to provide what they need in a fast and efficient way.

Zappos

Zappos makes shoe shopping fun and easy. Wrong size? No problem, return the shoes with free shipping and get your money back. Think about the reasons you love your favorite retailer. Besides quality and selection, service is probably high on the list. When you can't solve a problem yourself, Zappos offers a friendly, helpful customer service representative to set your mind at ease. Easy, efficient, trouble-free service develops loyalty in Zappos customers. This same type of customer loyalty can be developed in library users who are met with yes-focused staff committed to solving problems, who also have the support of their leadership to do so. At the heart of Zappos's successful customer service are its employees, who want to share the company's generous service and support with customers because they're invested in the company's success and believe in its guiding principles.

The largest online shoe retailer, Zappos was acquired in 2009 by Amazon, but its roots began in 1999 when Tony Hsieh got involved with Zappos as adviser and investor, followed by his successful rise to CEO. Hsieh's goal, to make the Zappos brand recognized for the best customer service, relies on staff, whom he calls the Customer Loyalty Team (CLT). The CLT contributed to developing Zappos's unique culture, because they were invited into the Zappos family during pivotal times in the company's growth, when big changes were required and the company faced major struggles.

Creating a dedicated team starts with including staff in changes that affect them. The "Zappos Culture Book"[8] comprises employees' contributions on what Zappos culture means to them. Employees are encouraged to submit their responses on what they like, what's different, and the meaning of the Zappos culture. Most of us have read online product reviews, and we may have written a few ourselves, but can you imagine writing a review of the company or library in which you work? In one hundred to five hundred words, employees are invited to virtually share with the world their feedback on working at Zappos. Nearly all of the uncensored responses claim loyalty to Zappos and describe a commitment to the company that makes going to work exciting and fun. The book is shared with all new hires at Zappos so they gain an understanding of their new workplace and can read the employees' stories about their loyalty to Zappos.

Zappos staff participate in the "Ask Anything" e-mail, which distributes the answers back to staff, who ask questions ranging from, "What other music have we considered having as our hold music?" and "What's the most expensive item we have ever had on our site?" Funny questions are not at all off limits: "Do vegetarians eat animal crackers?"[9] The success of Zappos can be attributed to leadership that invested in its culture, the customer experience, and the personal and professional development of its staff.[10] Staff get Zappos news in messages that describe the state of Zappos, and early on the company shared difficult messages with staff about financial struggles and its decision to move its headquarters to Las Vegas. When Zappos hit the 200,000 pairs of shoes sold mark, news went out to staff to both encourage and brag about the company at which they worked.

Although Zappos employees receive thousands of calls and e-mails daily, staff performance is never measured by the number of calls staff answer but rather by the quality of service the customer receives. Employees are expected to go above and beyond customer expectations in every transaction. The longest Zappos phone call was six hours long. Even though Zappos phone customers account for only about 5 percent of sales, Zappos uses phone conversations as a way to "create a lasting memory."[11] If library staff were to do the same—focus on customer opportunities rather than interruptions—how many more loyal customers would be reached?

Zappos lists ten ways to instill customer service. Applying Zappos's retail model for customer service to libraries would revolutionize their effectiveness in the communities libraries serve:

> 1) Make customer service a priority, not just a department. A customer service attitude needs to come from the top; 2) Make WOW a verb that is part of your company's everyday vocabulary; 3) Empower and trust your customer service reps. Trust that they want to provide great service . . . because they actually do. Escalations to a supervisor should be rare; 4) Realize that it's okay to fire customers who are insatiable or abuse your employees; 5) Don't measure call times, don't force employees to upsell, and don't use scripts; 6) Don't hide your 1-800 number. It's a message not just to your customers, but to your employees as well; 7) View each call as an investment in building a customer service brand, not as an expense you're seeking to minimize; 8) Have the company celebrate great service. Tell stories of WOW experiences to everyone in the company; 9) Find and hire people who are already passionate about customer service; 10) Give great service to everyone: customers, employees, and vendors.[12]

Zappos states that "your culture is your brand,"[13] which means its culture is built on transparency to customer responses. Consumers report their feedback to global shoppers via the Internet, whether they are unhappy or exceedingly grateful. Placing the emphasis on the customer experience and customer service made Zappos the success it is today. Hsieh writes, "At Zappos, our belief is that if you get the culture right, most of the other stuff—like great customer service, or building a long-term brand, or passionate employees and customers—will happen naturally on its own."[14] How can libraries invest in their brand through the development of their culture? Zappos does it by hiring people who fit into the culture it wants to achieve. People who have a passion for customer service are identified in the interview process. Questions are based not entirely on talent but on applicants' service to others. Sample interview questions at Zappos include: "What was the best mistake you made on the job? Why was it the best?" and "When was the last time you broke the rules/policy to get the job done?"[15] At Zappos everyone goes through the same training, in which the company's history, vision, and philosophy and the importance of customer service are presented. At the end of the first week of training, employees are offered $2,000 to quit (plus pay for time worked), an offer that can be seized up until the end of the fourth week of training, because as Hsieh describes, "We want to make sure that employees are here for more than just a paycheck."[16] If an employee can be lured into leaving the company for cash, Zappos would not want to retain that person. It retains the people who fit into the Zappos culture of customer service.

Developing a library culture of service takes time and must be created not by leadership but by the organization. It is based on trusting and empowering staff to act in the customer's favor.

Obviously, building a culture of customer service requires hiring the right people and communicating the company's plans and goals. Not surprising, Zappos believes that its best ideas come from those who are closest to the customers and the issues—from the bottom up. Team members collaborate on issues to resolve challenges and strive to create harmony. Yes, harmony in the workplace. Team members trust each other and believe in each other—they have each other's backs. It's no wonder the Zappos culture incubates so many great customer service representatives. Goals are clear, employees support each other, and everyone knows what's going on in the company. Teams are valued for their insights for solving problems. Since its "marriage" to Amazon, Zappos continues to make it onto the list of Fortune's 100 Best Companies to Work For.

The Ritz-Carlton Hotel Company

The Ritz-Carlton Hotel Company creates memorable experiences, connects with guests individually, and delivers service customized to guests' preferences.[17] The hotel creates legendary customer experiences based on the following five principles: "Define and Refine; Empower through Trust; It's Not about You; Deliver Wow; and Leave a Lasting Footprint."[18] The following section looks at the first four standards of Ritz-Carlton's premier customer service and provides inspiration for other businesses searching for the Ritz-Carlton gold standard for customer service.

The Ritz-Carlton continually defines and reviews the relevance of its products and services and evolves with customer trends. If a particular service no longer appeals to guests, the Ritz-Carlton updates its services. Public libraries can adopt a similar strategy by letting go of outdated policies and procedures that no longer reflect customer lifestyles. Ritz-Carlton staff are empowered to create unique, memorable, and personal experiences for their guests and are given the freedom to "own and immediately solve guest problems."[19] How many library staff are empowered to do the same? How many library customers get shuffled from person to person or sent off to another desk or black hole in the stacks? Memorable customized service is not exclusive to the luxury hospitality industry but can be used to create lifelong library customers as well.

Empowering through trust, the second of Ritz-Carlton's principles, once again leads to a premise it has in common with other successful businesses: customer service begins with hiring the right people. Searching for people who take pride in providing service is where it begins at Ritz-Carlton. The term "selection" is preferred over "hiring," for the simple reason that hiring is simply filling a job, while selection is choosing the "best person to provide exemplary service."[20] Staff make a commitment to responsibly meet the expectations of the trust placed in them. The process for getting hired at Ritz-Carlton is lengthy and requires several interviews by management and peers, but the investment in time for assessing job applicants increases the odds of identifying the right fit, enhances employee engagement and retention, and decreases staff turnover.[21] Staff are trained in Gold Standards over a twenty-one-day period ending in a certification process. New staff are embraced by a company culture that instills staff loyalty and provides empowerment for decision making. At the end of the twenty-one-day training, staff are encouraged to share their problems with the training department so they can be addressed. For library leaders, the takeaway in the Ritz-Carlton model is that when staff needs are met, that same type of attention and detail given to them can be passed on to customers. Take care of staff, and they will take care of customers.

Trust between leadership and staff must be mutual. Staff must trust leadership to provide the infrastructure for their employment, while leadership must trust staff to deliver on the services that increase customer satisfaction. Staff are not told what to do at Ritz-Carlton but are allowed to figure out what needs to be done in order to provide memorable guest experiences. Distrusting work environments set the stage for lack of empowerment for staff to make decisions in favor of the customer. These are the types of distrusting environments in which frontline staff are heard to say, "I will have to get my manager's approval on that."[22] How often do library staff call for backup on decisions that involve customer satisfaction? Again, we're not looking to build profits, but we are in the business of developing a strong customer base in order to ensure our relevance and reach in our communities. Allowing library staff to own customer problems and not shift the responsibility to another person creates immediate solutions and customer happiness. When customers are taken care of at the point of service, they see the trust the library places in staff and recognize they too are trusted. Immediately solving complaints leads to customer retention and growth. For Ritz-Carlton, empowerment through trust also means adding to the bottom line, and according to its research, results in significant financial benefits, numbering in the millions of dollars. The culture norm at Ritz-Carlton is based on serving others with extraordinary efforts. What can library leadership do to instill trust and empower staff to serve customers with extraordinary efforts in an environment of trust?

Ritz-Carlton not only sets out to deliver outstanding customer service and to build a culture of trust and staff empowerment, it also wants to keep its place as one of the industry's top employers. Ritz-Carlton measures the level of staff engagement through *Gallup Q12: Gallup's Employee Engagement Metric*,[23] an instrument that determines an employee's personal investment in the company. Employees fall into one of three categories: engaged, non-engaged, or actively disengaged, or in less lofty terms: owners, renters, or squatters.[24] Engaged employees are invested in the growth and success of Ritz-Carlton, whereas those who are actively disengaged—essentially squatters—are not. Engaged employees provide service that exceeds customer expectations. Ritz-Carlton rewards the employees who go above and beyond customer expectations by acknowledging them regularly. Because staff are empowered to create *wow* experiences, they are given allowances to meet guest needs on demand. It's not unusual for Ritz-Carlton employees to resolve guest problems or needs immediately, even if it involves shopping for an item that a guest forgot. Staff are empowered to make the Ritz-Carlton guest happy—they cover each other's absences when they need to leave the hotel to purchase something for a guest or provide a service to solve a problem. Employees make spontaneous decisions on demand. When a Ritz-Carlton employee receives a complaint, he or she is expected to own it completely by resolving and recording it. Ritz-Carlton gives freedom to its employees by trusting them to make decisions that create exceptional customer experiences, and it works.

Starbucks

Starbucks's growth depends on the connections employees make with the customer. Customer satisfaction alone is passé for today's thriving businesses. Customer service must be based on anticipating the customer's needs and is essential for customer loyalty to develop.

Starbucks bases its success on the delivery of friendly, customized service. It adheres to five principles that it describes as simple yet powerful: "Make it your own; Everything matters; Surprise and delight; Embrace resistance; and Leave your mark."[25] Providing anything but a scripted approach to customer service, Starbucks encourages employees to use their individuality to inspire customers. The "Five Ways of Being" provide employees with simple guidelines for creating legendary service: "Be welcoming; Be genuine; Be considerate; Be knowledgeable; Be involved."[26] How employees share their expressions of genuineness, consideration, knowledge, and involvement, and how they welcome customers, depends on the uniqueness of the employee. Starbucks wants its employees to personalize relationships with customers through meaningful connections based on surpassing customer requests. Employees are free to be themselves when given the opportunity, free from restrictive rules and boundaries.

Imagine being welcomed into a public library where staff genuinely and happily greet customers on arrival. Starbucks offers a genuine welcome, which gives customers a sense of belonging on arriving.[27] Once there, Starbucks customers enjoy a place that's neither work nor home—a "Third Place." Libraries can provide a Third Place and like Starbucks can offer people a place to relax, socialize, meet, and enjoy comfort outside of home and work.

Employee training at Starbucks includes scenarios that pose a dilemma, customer comment, attitude, or other cue for trainees to guess what might be going on inside of a customer's head.[28] Scenario training can prepare employees to respond to customers based on their observations or intuition, which is why it's so important the right people are hired. For Starbucks it's all about the details, which set its customer service apart from other businesses. A small detail may be the difference between success and failure, or dissatisfied customers.[29] Starbucks employees are encouraged to surprise and delight customers or even a coworker. The simple act of listening may be all that's required, or a simple gesture to let the customer know the company cares. Starbucks has a "just say yes"[30] policy, which allows employees the freedom to turn a customer request into a reality. Starbucks staff find workarounds to getting the customer what he or she wants if the requested drink is not listed on the menu. That's the type of personalized service that allows both the staff and customer to experience something good together.

The Walt Disney Company

Disney is in the business of creating happiness, and it couldn't be done without employing the right people dedicated to customized and responsive service. Disney guests enjoy courteous employees and are treated like VIPs—"a very important, very individual person."[31] It comes as no surprise that hiring the right people is imperative to Disney's success, as it is for other successful businesses. Disney seeks people with excellent interpersonal skills. Treating people the way they want to be treated, along with recognizing and respecting people of all backgrounds, abilities, and cultures, is key to Disney's attention to courtesy.[32] Memorable interactions with Disney employees are the single biggest factor in customer satisfaction and return visits.[33] The ability of Disney employees to connect with visitors contributes to its longevity among competitors. It really is all about the employees' ability to connect with Disney guests. Disney parks and resorts believe "our front line is our bottom line."[34] Disney is uniquely designed to welcome new staff into its culture, history, traditions, values, and behaviors, along with creating excitement about working for Disney, and safety regulations.[35] Disney's guidelines for guest services include (to name a few): make eye contact, a sincere smile, greet and welcome every guest, solve problems, display appropriate body language, and thank each and every guest.[36] Disney employees are encouraged to solve problems and find answers, and to use body language appropriately, by being attentive, maintaining good posture and pleasant facial expressions. Employees who speak and act sincerely essentially personalize the customer interaction. Culture at Disney, like at Starbucks, Zappos, and the other businesses included here, is based on employee individuality, buy-in from leadership to frontline staff, guidelines, training, staff feedback, and employee recognition.

Virgin Group

Sir Richard Branson, creator of the Virgin Group (Virgin Atlantic Airlines, Virgin Galactic, Virgin Megastores, Virgin Music, and Virgin Records), doesn't believe in entering a new market unless he has the potential to "shake up the industry."[37] Employees at Virgin Group companies are considered the business's greatest asset, and the company culture developed around delivering great customer service. Similar to other businesses that make long-term profits and growth, Branson believes that employees should be empowered to make decisions and create solutions when serving customers. Employees working in a friendly environment, one that is tolerant of mistakes, drive good customer service. Listening to staff, putting them first, and following up on their ideas and suggestions lead to the best solutions for the staff and customer. Blaming rules should not be part of a customer service response: "If your company is going to stand out from the rest because of its truly excellent customer service, staffers should treat the rules more as flexible guidelines, to be followed as the situation demands. The customer is not always right—and neither is the rulebook. The customer service representative's goal should be to strike a balance that serves both the customer's and company's interests in the best way possible."[38] When staff are encouraged to use common sense and are trusted, their solutions will become more inventive over time. As a result, Branson suggests, employees will become more entrepreneurial within the business. When an employee uses "they" instead of "we" when referring to the company, that points to a communication problem within the organization. For libraries, that looks like: "They sent your library account to collections" or "They just started this new rule."

Library staff are the greatest asset in the organization. In any service-based organization, the employees not only represent the product but they often *are* the product. In Branson's discussion "Third Person Problems," he suggests: "A company's employees are its greatest asset, particularly in service-based operations where your people are your product. When a company fails to grasp this simple business tenet, the result is invariably an oppositional 'us and them' divide between management and front-staff."[39] Narrowing the gap between leadership and frontline staff allows trusting employees to act independently in their own way to treat customers as they would like to be treated.

Southwest Airlines

Herb Kelleher started Southwest Airlines in 1967 to provide affordable air service. Kelleher was a stickler for hiring the right people and believed in the motto, "hire for attitude; train for skill."[40] Like other entrepreneurial leaders, Kelleher believes that customers always come first and that employees should be treated right. At the center of the equation are the customers, who will come back to use the service when they are treated right. Selecting the right people was what Kelleher referred to as a religion. If the company had to interview more than one hundred people for a ramp-agent position to find the right person, it would. Kelleher believed that the most important thing is to get the right people, because if you get the wrong ones, "they can start poisoning everybody else."[41] Kelleher, like other business leaders, focused on getting customers what they wanted and not on profit margins. Employees were told, "Don't worry about profit. Think about customer service."[42] Kelleher said, "Profit is a by-product of good customer service. It's not an end in and of itself."[43]

Public library employees provide intrinsic services beyond the scope of products and services; the lives of library customers are changed as a result of dedicated staff who connect them with information, ideas, and inspiration.[44] From the elderly woman struggling at the public workstation to fill out government forms, to the man slowly tapping key by key to finish a job application, these are a few of the people who rely on library staff for essential help—help that directly affects their quality of life.[45]

Knowing what library products and services to offer customers is key to providing personalized service. A cache of resources exists within the library from which to make the best customer selection. The extent to which customer satisfaction is met depends on the depth of staff awareness of every possibility the library offers. Personalized solutions are met when staff reach into their cache of expertise and draw out enticing options. Staff will not be able to connect with library customers unless they understand all of the options. Because the customer may not know exactly what he or she wants or what is available, it's imperative that staff be able to identify options and cross-promote in order to surpass customer expectations. When staff are excited about suggesting a new library service or material, customers will also respond with excitement. Only after a rapport is built with the customer at the desk, on the phone, or at the other end of the chat or e-mail will we truly connect with customer needs in a personal way. Staff who provide this level of service are often those who are remembered by customers and requested by name. If customers ask for a specific staff person by name, you can be sure a personal connection was made through exceptional service. Surprised and delighted customers find inspiration and ideas by connecting with library staff, who suggest appealing choices based on the customer's expressed interests. Finally, listening is the key to making customer connections. Move the routine transaction from mundane to "wow" by listening and offering feedback based on what's heard.

Distilling this advice from leaders who changed the way the world does business provides libraries with a roadmap of possibilities:

Frontline staff:
- Create happiness and exceptional customer experiences.
- Be yourself and allow your personality to shine.
- Be friendly.
- Throw away customer service scripts.
- Walk customers to the destination.
- Invite customers to enjoy the library as a Third Place.

Leadership:
- Hire the right people.
- Invite staff into the library culture immediately after hiring them.
- Trust and empower staff to make the decisions that exceed customer expectations; customer satisfaction is no longer the norm.
- Take care of staff, and they will take care of customers.
- Increase communication and listen to frontline staff.
- Allow staff to make mistakes.
- Set the stage for a service culture that encourages solutions and innovation.

Business models teach us that customer service employees are the essential link to personalized service, and the customer will always respond positively to staff seeking to customize solutions in order to surpass expectations. Looking to businesses that have invested heavily in developing customized service, based not only on what the customer seeks but beyond anything the customer can imagine, provides a simple roadmap for public libraries to follow. It begins with hiring the right people, ensuring that staff understand all of the products and services the library offers, and training staff to implement the soft skills—essentially the human connection—required to build customer satisfaction and loyalty to the public library.

NOTES

1. Kathy Middleton, "The Answer Is Yes," *Public Libraries* 54, no. 1 (January/February 2015): 11.

2. Neiman Marcus, "The Neiman Marcus Group, Careers," https://www.neimanmarcuscareers.com/story/mission.shtml.

3. Neiman Marcus, "The Neiman Marcus Group: Corporate Mission," https://www.neimanmarcuscareers.com/story/mission.shtml.

4. Robert Spector and Patrick McCarthy, *The Nordstrom Way* (Hoboken, NJ: John Wiley & Sons, 2005), 6–7.

5. Ibid.

6. Ibid., 27.

7. "Nordstrom, Inc. SWOT Analysis" (November 2015): 5, Business Source Complete, EBSCOhost (accessed February 12, 2015).

8. Zappos, "2014 Culture Book," http://www.zapposinsights.com/culture-book/digital-version/download-cb.

9. Tony Hsieh, *Delivering Happiness* (New York: Business Plus, 2010), 136.

10. Ibid., 137.

11. Ibid., 145.

12. Ibid., 147.

13. Ibid., 152.

14. Ibid.

15. Ibid., 172.

16. Ibid., 152.

17. Joseph A. Michelli, *The New Gold Standard: 5 Leadership Principles for Creating a Legendary Customer Experience Courtesy of The Ritz-Carlton Hotel Company* (New York: McGraw Hill, 2008), 147.

18. Ibid., 15.

19. Ibid., 64–65.

20. Ibid., 76.

21. Ibid., 79.

22. Ibid., 109–110.

23. Ibid., 127.

24. Ibid.

25. Joseph A. Michelli, *The Starbucks Experience* (New York: McGraw-Hill, 2007), 16.

26. Ibid., 20–21.

27. Ibid., 22.

28. Ibid., 68.

29. Ibid., 79.

30. Ibid., 144.

31. Disney Institute and Theodore B. Kinni, *Be Our Guest* (New York: Disney Editions, 2011), 49.

32. Ibid.

33. Ibid., 61.
34. Ibid.
35. Ibid., 66.
36. Ibid., 73.
37. Richard Branson, *Like a Virgin* (New York: Penguin, 2012), 43.
38. Ibid., 210.
39. Ibid., 49.
40. Richard Branson, *The Virgin Way* (New York: Penguin Group, 2014), 229.
41. John A. Byrne, *World Changers* (New York: Penguin Group, 2011), 78.
42. Branson, *The Virgin Way*, 229.
43. Ibid.
44. Middleton, "The Answer Is Yes," 12.
45. Ibid.

5

Eliminate *No*

Public library service must begin with the simple practice of saying "yes" far more often than "no." All too often, "no" blocks essential library services and drives customers away from public libraries toward easier, friendlier, and more accessible businesses to find the resources they seek. Certainly library staff would not intentionally block access to any library product or service—we are, after all, champions for intellectual freedom and public access—yet when asked to clear obstacles that block customer access, we often cite outdated policies or procedures embedded in "no." Obstacles such as these prove difficult for customers, causing frustration, anger, and shame. When staff are empowered by library leaders to say "yes" and are granted the freedom to provide more choices, customers are amazed and overjoyed.

This chapter defines the urgent need for excellent customer service strategies in libraries and why "yes" is so much easier for staff to accomplish than "no." Library staff have grown accustomed to saying "no" over the years as policies and procedures continued to grow more complex in an attempt to provide fairness and equity. The idea of focusing on "yes" for all customer transactions requires a shift in thinking by library leadership first, followed by staff empowerment to make decisions in favor of the customer. Rather than asking staff to adhere to procedures for one-size-fits-all transactions, the focus for service must be repositioned on product and service knowledge as a toolbox into which to reach for offering personalized choices. This is in contrast to training staff to adhere to unreasonable procedures and unbendable rules that drive customers away. Customers often cannot, or will not, comply with rigid library rules when so many other convenient, easy, and yes-delivered options are available.

Perceptions of the stereotypical librarian portrayed in books and movies are slowly disappearing, but still the following stereotypes persist:

Librarians:
- Shush and enforce quiet
- Read all day long and think they're smarter than anyone else
- Wear sturdy, sensible shoes
- Wear eyeglasses
- Delight in enforcing rules
- Say "no"
- Try to catch people in the act of wrongdoing
- Sit for long periods of time and don't like to be interrupted
- Have few responsibilities other than enforcing rules

Some stereotypical librarian behavior originates in truth. Library staff communicate customer "nos" through rules, policies, and everyday procedures. Others originate from staff attitudes, inflexibility, and adherence to practices from years ago. If the public library were in the profit-making arena and depended on customer service to turn revenue, how long would the library stereotypes continue to exist?

For the sake of comparison, libraries can be folded into the service industry category. Public libraries provide goods and services to the public for consumption. Service to customers drives the mission, vision, and goals of libraries, so it makes sense to borrow observations, studies, and reports from those who measure satisfaction in the service industry. For example, a 2011 American Express study found that fewer than one in ten customers report that customer service exceeded their expectations, which means most customers are not getting the service they want.[1] "Customers have become accustomed to being abused by the companies they buy services from. Their expectations are low, low, low. The most hated companies, and the most hated industries are service providers."[2] The authors of the study report that customers will resist standardization, meaning customer demands cannot be met without personalizing service. Their needs will not fit into standard boxes; that's when the customer becomes frustrated and angry.[3] As library service providers embrace practices that allow personalized service, which includes listening, assessing need, and offering custom solutions, library customers will add libraries to their list of "yes" service providers.

SIGNS OF "NO"

Late materials require fines, lost items must be paid for, holds must be picked up or customers may incur fees—these are a few of the financial consequences associated with library policy. Customers who complain about such policies and perceived unfairness are often thought of as troublemakers, instigators, and problem patrons, when they are simply voicing their dissatisfaction, particularly in light of companies (Zappos, Starbucks, Ritz-Carlton, etc.) that know how to immediately satisfy customer requests.

Library staff may argue that it's unfair to waive fines for some customers and not others. One size does not fit all. Customized solutions require customized transactions. If a library fine is blocking a customer's access because an item wasn't returned when the customer was ten years old almost twenty years ago, can we agree to forgive the fine and create a loyal library customer? Staff may suggest that customers are "scamming the library" if fines are waived. In response to that argument, I point out that customers who consistently behave irresponsibly are in the minority, and as such should be handled on an individual basis. The majority of library customers whose fines have climbed to the level of blocked access should not be penalized forever. Individual circumstances should be handled individually based on the customer's personal situation, and with leniency.

In the end it comes down to listening to the customer and finding a way to exceed expectations. Businesses dedicated to developing loyal customers provide them with easy, simple rules, so small they fit on a register receipt. In contrast, public library rules fill walls and desks and reside within the layers of the virtual library. A high percentage of public library customer complaints are reasonable and accurate, if we will allow ourselves to recognize that fact through a yes-focused lens.

The information desk can be one of the most formidable obstacles blocking customers, both physically and psychologically, from resources and services. The desk is a fortress and blocks frontline staff from fully engaging with customers. It creates an "us against them" environment. The service desk looks less intimidating when (1) extraneous materials are cleared away; (2) staff look approachable through their body language; (3) staff provide a warm welcome; (4) staff have the desire to listen; and (5) staff abandon the desk regularly in favor of making personal customer connections. Regardless of desk size or type, staff who look approachable and ready to help are already improving access. A desk cleared of clutter helps eliminate distractions for the customer so he or she can focus on communicating the information request. If staff are the most important resource in the library (I certainly believe they are!), they are all that's needed to provide the best customer experience ever. It's not necessary to eliminate printed and displayed materials altogether, but they should be in an area that is easily accessed by both customers and staff when needed.

Customers don't read signs. No matter how many are posted, or their location, size, or attractiveness, signs rarely inform library customers. Even when the library is closed and the lights are off, a closed sign will not deter people from pulling on the door or peeking in. Signs cannot replace a personal response to a customer's need. A sign can be placed on the desk with all of the information a customer needs, but for customers, it's easier to ask and get answers by means of conversation.

No-focused signs create barriers and give the impression that visitors are unwelcome. Signs are evidence that a particular behavior is not acceptable. "Stop," "Don't," and "Wrong" magnified on a sign make a firm statement and send a message equivalent to "You are not welcome here." Retail businesses building customers and profit rarely post signs that blatantly communicate "no." Outside of the public library, signs that correct customer behavior are often associated with the U.S. Postal Service, the Department of Motor Vehicles, and other governmental agencies. Visits to bureaucratic agencies require a special set of rules, procedures, and practices, which in many ways are similar to public library rules. "Take a ticket" and "Wait here," both communicate, "Customer beware: You are in for a negative experience." Behavior-based signage promotes a negative response and perpetuates the stereotypical library and librarian images. For example, "No cell phones," "No beverages," "No talking," "No entrance," "No sleeping," "No, No, No!" are all behavioral instructions aimed at the small percentage of customers who act outside the norms. Of course libraries need rules, but why penalize all library visitors for the few who cannot act appropriately in a public place? Sometimes posted library rules become ridiculous and unreasonable, and others are an expression of airing library dirty laundry: "No weapons," "No illegal activity," "No physical assaults," "No tobacco products," "No sexual activity," "No body odor," and "No alcohol or illegal drugs." What do these rules proclaim to customers? They suggest that libraries are rife with crime and violence and deal with the infractions listed on a regular basis. Chapter 1 mentioned that we deal swiftly and appropriately with behavior problems by not allowing customers inside who interfere with the use of the library. If public libraries swiftly and appropriately remove and ban patrons who commit unlawful acts, the customers who want to enjoy the library will be served.

Rules of conduct should be posted, but they do not need to be posted on every desk and wall in the library—besides, how many patrons are legitimately ignorant of the law or devoid of conscience? Most people inherently know how to behave in a public place. A sign will not curtail bad behavior. Consequently, libraries must rely on more than posted library rules to address behavioral problems. Such problems must be addressed quickly, consistently, and effectively by all staff.

Signs are frequently overused and unread, but let's take a moment to enjoy some creatively phrased signs posted in real libraries that communicate "no." Ridiculous signs were the subject of John Brandon's "9 Very Specific Rules from Real Libraries," published in *Mental Floss*.[4] Undoubtedly the general public became more convinced after reading Brandon's article that libraries are trying harder than ever to communicate "no." The article included photos of outrageous library signs captured at nine libraries that warned visitors to keep the door closed during meetings so bats could not enter the building, against bringing balloons inside, and to keep clothing zipped. Problems with children chewing on headphone cords? Post a sign to prevent such mischief, as displayed by another library that Brandon described. Signs like these are probably not read by the person creating the problem, but by others, who find them confusing, or more probably, immersed in "no." Library staff love to create signs. Most have created a sign or two with the intention of solving an irritating problem but will still find themselves speaking to customers about the problem described on the sign. Signs should not be used to replace a person-to-person conversation. No-focused signs are created for the minority of visitors who do not behave appropriately in the public library, not for the majority of visitors who simply want to locate a resource, use a computer, attend a program, read, or study. Signage will not prevent people from doing what's posted. People who follow standard norms of conduct do not need to read rules, and those who do not follow norms of behavior neither read nor adhere to rules. Rules of conduct do not discourage bad behavior and should not be overdone by posting them everywhere. They should be made available on a small card that can be shared with customers as needed. A single sign is all that's needed for a library or library floor. When libraries provide a respectful environment for the majority of library customers, the number of signs needed is minimal.

The Apple Store is a perfect example of the minimalist aesthetic that gives customers think space. The Apple Store environment allows customers and staff to focus on the product without the distractions of excessive signage. Excess library signage is the equivalent to digital ads and irritating pop-ups online. They are overwhelming and annoying, and customers do not want to be bombarded with messaging. They expect what retailers know they must deliver: an environment in which to browse, explore, and find products that they need or discover that they need while browsing.

Attitude

Library customers are the most important aspect of daily library work, but sometimes customers are treated poorly. Customers may view staff as computer cops, fee mavens, and "shushers." How can staff meet the needs of a customer struggling with an online application for minimum wage employment? Assisting people with online job applications will eliminate a negative response and could actually contribute to the economic prosperity of the library community—when someone finds employment. The public library is often the only place where a customer can turn to find job-seeking help. Businesses that are hiring often refer job applicants to public libraries, as well as to state unemployment offices. Making time for a customer at the point of need will ensure that he or she has the opportunity to submit a job application, learns how to repeat the process, and ultimately looks to the library for lifelong resources. Focusing on outcomes such as academic or job success produces outcomes. Outcomes that change lives should always be considered along with outputs that provide important statistics but don't adequately reflect improvements in customers' lives.

Cat Fithian, Library Branch Supervisor

A man was demanding a lot of attention from staff to build his résumé, save it, get an e-mail account, and e-mail his résumé to a potential employer. Another staff member came to me to warn me or perhaps to complain about him. When it was my shift on the desk, I was up next to help him. I noticed that he spoke English with a thick accent. In reviewing his résumé, his high school diploma was from a technical school rather than an academic degree. He was extremely anxious about using the computer, and much of his information on the résumé builder he was trying to use was poorly formatted, with misspelled words.

Also, the résumé builder he'd found through the Google search my staff instructed him to use had led him to a pay-for-use site where you may build the résumé but must pay to be able to save or even e-mail it. No wonder he was frustrated! I sat down, introduced myself, and asked if it would be OK if I retyped his information. I opened a WORD document, retyped his sparse information, formatted it, and checked with him along the way to be sure that we had all the addresses he could remember. Then we set up a new Gmail account, as he couldn't remember his old passwords. I got him a small piece of notepaper and he wrote down his new e-mail address and password to keep in his wallet. Then I saved the résumé to Google Drive for him and e-mailed it to the potential employer. Then we had a little conversation about how that guy will probably get back to him by e-mail, and if he wants to know if he's got an interview, he's going to need to check his e-mail. I told him that if he ever needs help again, he can come back.

Personalize Help

How do we welcome people who are unfamiliar with navigating the library? Visitors who do not speak English, or those who are visiting for the first time, will not automatically know library practices. The idea that a public library is a *free* resource may also be unfamiliar. Because public libraries have specific ways of handling, for example, computer use or book borrowing, it's important to orient first-time visitors when they request a library card. A few simple words of welcome, and whenever possible taking the time to demonstrate how to use the self-service machines, or simply inviting the customer to feel free to ask any questions, will provide a sincere welcome. Customizing the welcome will depend on the need of the customer. A respected library colleague always asks new customers, "What brought you to the library today?" This open-ended question invites a conversation and gets at what the customer is seeking.

For example, an elderly customer needs assistance with online forms: With great effort, she lumbers through the library door, relying on a squeaky walker to make her way to the service desk. Breathing as if she'd walked miles already, she quietly states that she needs help with an online form and shares her frustration with failing eyesight and old age. Her arthritic hands can no longer hold a pen for long, and keyboarding takes great effort. The response from library staff is usually one of three things: (1) "I wish I could help you, but I can't. We don't have enough staff"; (2) "I can get you started on the computer, but after that you're on your own"; or (3) "I can make an appointment for you to come back and meet with a computer volunteer." If we acknowledge that staff are the most important resource in the library, and customer loyalty is essential for the future of the library, then can we agree to provide backup staff who will come out from the staff room to help with one-on-one service? If, for example, the elderly woman has basic computer skills, it may be possible for her to complete a portion of the form; however, if she is sent off on her own to log-in, find the form, fill in the blanks, and submit it, she will probably become frustrated and either ask for help multiple times or leave the library disappointed and without completing the form. She will either return the next day to try again, look for people in her life who can help her, or give up completely.

It's very likely that during your workday you encounter adults who cannot read, even in the library. Ashamed and embarrassed to admit it, adults who cannot read often don't tell their families. At the library service desk, staff might hear: "I forgot my glasses; can you read that part to me?" Adults with low reading skills will need help to fill out a form or apply for a job online, and they hide the fact that they cannot read. If staff can provide assistance by referring the customer to an adult literacy program when appropriate or listening for cues to remedy the need, libraries will be much closer to achieving positive outcomes and a new relevance in people's lives.

Most of us assume that all teens grow up with and possess technological skills, but there are teens who lack basic computer competencies. Many teens do not have a computer or Internet access at home, do not own a smartphone, or do not have any way to produce homework apart from the technology the public library offers. Some teens are embarrassed they do not know how to save files, create reports in Word, or prepare a PowerPoint presentation that's expected for class. That's why it's so important we don't make assumptions that youth are tech-savvy or automatically possess technology skills. Technology gaps occur across all ages and in all socioeconomic spheres. Library staff have no way of knowing a customer's skill level, so it's crucial for library staff to listen to the customer's requests and respond accordingly. For example, the principal of a K–8 school where 88 percent of the students live below the poverty level praised the public library for helping students. Because those students depend on the public library for computer access after school, and because students rely on homework help, the principal praised the neighborhood library as a vital component in academic success, which she believes has the potential to lead students to a future without poverty.[5]

Turn "No" into "Yes"

How can libraries turn "nos" into "yeses"? Are we too busy to help? What is the worst thing that can happen as a result of giving people what they want? It's time to turn the focus away from processes and behaviors that distract from what's needed. Sometimes, in an effort to be fair and consistent and create unilateral service standards, we skip personalized service altogether. Today's customers enjoy choices that are easy and hassle free. We would not willingly block customers from accessing any material or service, but we continue to hang on to rigid procedures that impede library service and access. Building a loyal customer base of satisfied people results in changed lives.

Change begins when we adopt a new attitude toward customized service. It's more important than our intellectual or technological skills or our knowledge of Dewey Decimal or Library of Congress classification systems. The customer conversation, the interaction—often it's the "us against them" mentality when it comes to staff responses. Only when we connect with "them" do we add to our ability to be relevant and accessible for people in our communities. What we as customers usually remember is very bad service or exceptional service.

Inclusivity

People with intellectual and developmental disabilities (I/DD) visit public libraries every day with community-based groups. Some libraries are eliminating barriers by providing welcoming programs that start with library tours, introductions to staff, and monthly programs aimed at improving life skills and opportunities for lifelong learning. "Library Insiders" programs were developed first at Contra Costa County (CA) Library[6] and expanded to other community libraries. Recently Library Insiders programs were added to two Sacramento public libraries, then expanded to libraries in San Jose, and now they also exist in libraries outside California, in Kentucky, Colorado, and Missouri. Adults with I/DD are being welcomed into libraries through a variety of programs and services created to break down attitudinal barriers.

Library Insiders

Programs for Adults with I/DD, Chris Gray, Librarian

The Danville Library started its Insiders program almost two years ago, and in that time I've come to know many participants by name and have even engaged some in ways I think are fulfilling to us both. Peter visits the library daily with his educational/activity group, and when staff first noticed him, it was because he wandered around aimlessly, sometimes staring at other patrons. After I talked to him directly, I found that he craved interaction and wanted to share his unique ideas for inventions. On a given day, he might ask me if I'd ever thought of, say, a "helium magnet" as a Christmas gift for children, and I'd ask him questions about the magnet and how it works. Now we have an interactive relationship in which he draws cryptic diagrams and schematics of his engineering ideas, and I brainstorm with him on how they can be used or improved. I can tell that he is excited to have someone to share his ideas with, and I find the ideas and interactions fascinating and fun. By engaging in a "different" kind of patron dynamic, we've both improved our library experience in ways that I couldn't have anticipated.

Jennifer Harmonson, Librarian

Having grown up with an older brother with intellectual and developmental disabilities, I thought starting programs for this segment of our population would come naturally to me and that I would have the least personal "takeaway" from it. I could not have been more wrong! Starting the Library Insiders at Sacramento Public Library has provided a stark reminder that there is no one-size-fits-all for any of the patrons we serve. Where I am accustomed to a man four years my senior who will forever be on a parallel with the typical seven-year-old, some of the participants in the monthly programs are so high-functioning that it took me more than one session to fully determine who are the students and who are the teachers! The core group comes from an adult transitioning program at a local high school.

Sensory Storytimes

In addition to libraries welcoming adults with disabilities, Sensory Storytime programs welcome children with disabilities, particularly children on the autism spectrum, along with their families, to relax and feel comfortable during storytime. Families and children of all abilities are invited, but Sensory Storytimes provide an environment built on flexibility. Children can respond to stories, visual schedules, and interactive play in an environment of acceptance and inclusion. Parents of children with autism often hesitate to attend routine storytimes for fear their child will behave outside of program guidelines and expectations, so provide a storytime in which expectations are flexible and inclusive, so children can experience stories without normal restrictions. Sensory Storytimes provide opportunities for children to explore, speak out, and experience the delight of a story, engage in crafts, or simply play with a "fidget toy" provided for their comfort.

Janet Wininger, Librarian

What Sensory Storytime means to parents of autistic kids

- Provides a place for families of kids with special needs to feel welcome in the library and included. Many parents love libraries but fear bringing their ASD kids due to behaviors and stares from other patrons and staff.
- Provides library services directly addressing the child's special needs . . . abilities as well as disabilities.
- Gives parents a chance to network with other parents, sharing information and creating relationships.
- Accommodates a large range of differences in kids, with resources such as sensory toys for fidgets, activities targeted to visual learners, and personal attention from our staff in getting to know each child.
- Promotes tolerance and acceptance of those with special needs by offering significant exposure to Sensory Programs, which is good for all library staff.

What Sensory Storytime means to parents who attend with kids who don't have disabilities

- Creates happiness in parents of "typical" kids because their child may have behavior issues or lack attention skills. Their children may be visual learners even if not diagnosed with a disability.
- Accepts children who have difficulty sitting through a regular storytime, or children who can only follow books by hearing them read aloud.
- Helps typical children gain experience with peers with ASD: practicing cooperation and gaining a better understanding of those with special needs. Nearly one in forty-five kids is now being diagnosed on the autism spectrum.
- Engages children more than traditional storytime; it promotes participation and good group skills, all of which will be helpful in a child's educational future.

Inclusive programs are the ultimate in yes-focused activities that a library can provide. When considering programs for library customers, keep in mind that people with disabilities can enjoy the same programs and be engaged in the same activities as everyone else. Programs such as Sensory Storytimes and Library Insiders provide additional opportunities for people without disabilities and staff who learn more about connecting with people who are different than themselves. Inclusive programs promote tolerance and acceptance for all library customers. Many wonderful librarians dedicate themselves to people with special needs and share that leading inclusive programs has been the most rewarding part of their library careers.

AVOID "NO"

The best way to avoid saying "no" is to offer the customer choices. Be aware of all the options and how to talk about them. An innovative library supervisor wanted to learn more about why yes-focused service couldn't always be offered and created a "no log" or "customer obstacles log." The log provided feedback for ways to improve the customer experience by listing the transactions that resulted in "no."

"No" Responses

General:
- *I'm new to my job.*
- *I'll get in trouble with my supervisor.*
- *I'm not allowed to make those kinds of decisions on my own.*
- *I don't have time to find ways to say "yes."*
- *It's easier to treat all customers the same.*
- *I don't like working with the public. I was transferred here from another department.*
- *I have so much other work to do that I'm constantly distracted when I staff the public desk.*
- *I'm not confident in my own skills.*
- *I'm often tired and lack energy when I staff the desk.*
- *I'm scheduled to work with the public for five hours straight.*
- *I'm often stressed out by customer requests.*
- *I don't enjoy interacting with people.*
- *Customers are rude, angry, insensitive, and insulting and may act entitled.*

- *Customers don't usually appreciate any extra effort, so why should I go the extra mile?*

Information (Reference) and Referral:
- *We don't have that book. You will have to put that title on hold. It will take three to five days to arrive here.*
- *All the books for the book club are checked out. Maybe you can come to next month's book club, but you will need to be one of the first ten people to sign up since we have limits on attendance.*

Circulation:
- *You owe $5.25 in late fines.*
- *This book is lost? You will have to pay $26.95, plus a late fee of $6.50, plus a processing fee of $5.00. If you don't pay, the debt will be sent to a collection agency.*
- *Your hold expired, and it's not here any longer; and no, I don't know what book was sent back because we don't keep track of patron records.*
- *Your card is blocked!*
- *A replacement card will cost you $2.00.*
- *Since you didn't bring your library card, I need your photo ID to check out this book, even though you come in every day and I know who you are.*

Digital and Technology Service:
- *We cannot extend your time on the computer. Everyone gets one hour; that's it.*
- *We cannot help you with that; it will take too much time! I can get you started at the computer, but then you'll be on your own.*

Programs:
- *No storytimes this week. We are happy you've grown accustomed to attending, but we need to interrupt the program because we need to take a break.*
- *We are presenting programs that are of interest to the librarians. We hope they will interest the public too.*

Special Populations:
- *We don't have many assistive technologies for people with disabilities. The equipment and software we have rarely get used, and I don't know how to use them either.*
- *We don't have books that are easy to read for adults with learning disabilities. They can go to the children's area.*

Customer Obstacles Log, Thomas Gruneisen,
Branch Supervisor

The idea of keeping a "Customer Obstacles Log" was simple, and in many ways it was an extension of the increasingly common customer service practice of keeping a "No Log," or list of occurrences in which a customer's request is refused. In this iteration, staff were asked to notice and log not only sources of customer friction that resulted in a "hard no," but also those that could have resulted in that outcome, or which were simply observed to have negatively impacted our customers' experiences at the library. In this way, we found the Customer Obstacles Log to be a more aggressive tool in terms of identifying sources of customer friction, resulting in benefits that were both expected and unforeseen.

As anticipated, asking staff to capture experiences that fall short of a "hard no" helped in identifying restrictive practices that had faded into the background over time, bringing them back to the fore, where they could be reevaluated. It also revealed passive sources of customer discontent, ranging from a lack of parking to how our DVDs were shelved. This feedback allowed us to alter some in-branch practices and facility configurations, as well as to identify broader practices rooted in policy whose alteration would require the approval of our governing body. To shift the Customer Obstacles Log from an exercise that occurred mainly with pen and paper to one that encouraged more active staff involvement, these observations, as well as their collaboratively discovered solutions, were discussed both at one-on-one supervisor-direct meetings, as well as at our weekly staff meetings, and in the future will be rolled out at larger regional meetings.

More important, however, the Customer Obstacles Log placed our customers' experiences back at the center of our awareness, increasing staff sensitivity while providing a natural mechanism for continuous improvement. The act of logging sources of friction itself raised staff awareness of our customers, while its follow-up discussion helped ensure accountability and participation across staff. It also gave us a way to talk openly about customer service, allowing us to discuss library policies as well as personal practices, leading not just to innovation but also to consistency. Some leading practices had already been implemented at the branch but were being exercised unevenly by different staff; in other cases, it helped staff to collaboratively develop a "tool kit" of responses to various scenarios. Finally, these discussions provided an avenue for staff to recognize and congratulate themselves on good customer service, promoting a culture that prizes the ability to say "yes" to our customers.

"Nos" on the Network

Gray and Vander Wal (2012) provide reasons for companies to recognize the power of connected customers along with the enormous changes in doing business that social networks have created. Instantaneous tweets and posts can bring doom or praise to our doorsteps. The power of customers to choose what to buy has always been there, along with the sharing of customer buying experiences, but today those buying customers can quickly connect globally and broadcast their experiences to the world.[7] Even though direct dollars aren't being spent on library products and services, the power of comments online can affect library use.

Yelp reviews are powerful! A Nielson study reported that 90 percent of customers trust recommendations from other customers more than any other form of advertising.[8] Follow up on the local library's Yelp reviews and comments whenever possible. Social networking has changed the way people view restaurants, retail businesses, schools, and even public libraries. Libraries go to great expense presenting attractive and effective public Web pages, but customers look to each other when planning library visits. When customers want to get information about a restaurant, hotel, movies, or vacation, they turn to fast, easy answers on Yelp! Netflix, IMBD, Priceline, or Hotels.com. Customers trust their own and other customers' opinions and will seek answers that are quick, easy, and simple to understand.

Social media can support the library's message, indicate any shifts in customer opinion, and develop customer loyalty. Friends rely on social media to stay current and connect with new ideas, products, or services. Twitter, Facebook, Instagram, and other services provide a place for friends to share, suggest, and weigh in. Social media are where libraries need to meet customers. Social media platforms will change over time, but the connection that social media inspire will hold. For immediate communication, directness, and transparency, customers will consult social media.

Library customers want fast, efficient, and hassle-free service. Until libraries say "yes" many more times than "no," libraries will lose customers to yes-focused enterprises that provide similar library products and services. The customer who resists paying a late fee or who is wrongly accused of losing a book and forced to pay for it will go to Barnes and Noble or log on to Amazon to purchase a book in order to avoid negative or costly library transactions. When customer demand outweighs the library's ability to respond, customers will look elsewhere to find the materials they need. Poor customer service, lack of product and service knowledge, and lack of staff empowerment result in unhappy customers.

Finding ways to get to "yes" gives customers more options to choose from than ending transactions in a negative way. Gaining new library customers, luring back previous library customers, and growing a robust customer base require consistent, positive, and informed customer service. Personalizing library service brings the value-added retail component to customer service that resonates with consumers, to ensure the relevance and future of the library.

Staff may be resistant to change, and without support from library administrators the effects of "no" will persist and bar customers from library service and materials. Saying "yes" is much easier than ending conversations with "no."

Public Library Yelp Comments

Yelp comments can be scary to read, especially about the library in which you work, but be brave and read them with the intention to admit when mistakes were made and examine how you've rectified the problem. Most libraries receive negative reviews from time to time, but you should address the comments quickly and correct any mistaken perceptions. There are always two sides to a complaint, and people will continue to view the comments, so it's best to set the record straight. Many of the one-star Yelp reviews specifically point to staff as the major point of irritation. One comment described a library staff person as surly and rude. The reviewer described feeling like a criminal when she went to the library to get a card, and she was shuffled from person to person, each of whom she said was neither pleasant nor knowledgeable. Library customers read reviews before visiting libraries for information on what to expect, so it's important to meet our customers where they are on Yelp and reply as soon as possible to comments.

Yelp Comment by Bill S.

Today, I had a book on hold. I received an e-mail from the system alerting me that the book on hold was ready. I went to pick up the book, and asked the librarian if I could get it. She couldn't find it on the shelf, and asked when I received the e-mail. I told her that I received it about an hour ago. She rudely told me that I came in too early, and it takes a while to put held books on the shelf. Hmmmmm. . . . Stupid me. I stupidly assumed that the book was ready since I received an e-mail. She curtly told me, next time, don't come until much later.[9]

Customers who are picking up holds are probably regular library customers. Bill S. is not a customer the library wants to lose. Bill received an e-mail alert that the specific book he placed on hold was ready to pick up at his library branch. He went to the library and asked the person at the desk if he could pick it up after going to the hold shelf and not finding it there. The staff member asked Bill when he received notification that the hold was ready, and Bill reported that he'd received the e-mail about an hour earlier. The staff member rudely replied that the customer came in too early to pick up the book, because it takes time to get the hold books on the shelf. As a result, Bill was confused and annoyed, because he followed the directions given by the hold notification—to pick up the hold. If a customer takes the time to make a library trip after being notified a hold has arrived, but staff have not had time to put the hold on the shelf, why don't staff search for the missing book, even if it takes time to locate it? Why encumber the customer with process-related challenges, which creates a negative library experience? More appalling yet was the response by the library staff member, instructing Bill that he should have come in much later than instructed by the hold prompt issued by the library itself. This is not customer service on demand. This is an example of arcane and unyielding customer service that drives customers away.

Yelp Comment by Tanya L.

The library itself is a beautiful building and gives off a Victorian feeling. However, some of the staff I came across were incredibly rude. They are poorly trained with costomer [sic] service and will speak on what is on their mind. I asked a simple question and was answered with the rudest response from two different woman [sic]. Horrible experience, and I am sure to never go there again! I hope upper management will realize the type of low feedback that was experienced.[10]

Tanya L. liked the Victorian look and feel of the library she visited, but she won't be returning because she was treated rudely by two library staff members. She wanted library administrators to know that she had a "horrible" customer service experience at the hands of staff, who she thought were poorly trained. The library did not provide a reply to Yelp and lost an opportunity to share with readers that the complaint was taken seriously by library administrators and dealt with. Everyone knows that libraries and other businesses are subject to negative customer service transactions, but publicly acknowledging the validity of a complaint and promising to try harder will set the record straight and perhaps bring back visitors who were warned off by the comment.

Yes-Focused Customer Service Statements

Public library customer service statements range widely, some being detailed and others too broad to mean much. Following are a few customer service statements (not an exhaustive list) that illustrate a commitment to staff empowerment to make decisions in favor of the customer. Each also recognizes that the customer experience can be enhanced by personalizing the transaction based on request or need. Solution-oriented customer service results from library leadership trusting staff to identify customer need and to select the appropriate product, service, or action that will result in surpassing what's expected. Following are just a few winning examples of customer service statements, which demonstrate the level of commitment by staff to providing the ultimate customer experience.

Meriden (CT) Public Library, Customer Service Statement

The Meriden Public Library strives to offer excellent library services to all. In addition to the quality of the facility and the collection, it is equally important that the library staff provide accurate, efficient, and friendly service at all times. Although we often view the patron as the "clientele," it is important to remember that the patron, as voter and taxpayer, is also the ultimate "boss." The customer services policy is the foundation for all staff interactions with the general public. All other library policies should be interpreted in light of the principles outlined below. Patrons should be treated as if they are the most important people in the world. They are! Judgment calls should always be made in the patron's favor. If you make a mistake, it should always be to the patron's advantage. You will not be penalized for errors made in good faith pursuit of this policy.[11]

Boise Public Library, Access to Library Services

Flexible library services are tailored to the individual customer, delivered how and where the customer is and evolving to meet changing customer needs and technologies. Customers are the highest priority. Policies and procedures are nonrestrictive, with the goal of improving access. Services, policies, and procedures are developed with customer input and experiences in mind.[12]

Lawrence (KS) Public Library, Customer Service Values

Service to library customers is based on the values of the organization rather than merely on rules and procedures. Service policies are based on the mission of the library and the shared organizational values. Certain general concepts of values-based service differ from a service that is based solely on policies and procedures. . . . Empowerment: Staff members are encouraged to make decisions that will result in success for library customers. This means that anyone, not just a supervisor, can make an exception to policy or procedure if it provides quality customer service and is consistent with our organizational values. Customers like to have their problems solved by the first staff person with whom they deal. Staff members should feel confident and comfortable in solving individual problems.[13]

Customer Service Policy, Monroe County (IN) Public Library

We care about all of our customers and seek to give each one attentive service. . . . We seek out innovative approaches to serve our customers in the best ways possible.[14]

Responding to the customer's perspective and trusting staff to make decisions is essential for creating a yes-focused, personalized customer service model. Library staff should be allowed to exercise judgment on the customer's behalf, and this needs to be done in the moment, rather than asking for assistance from a supervisor. Personalizing service is being responsible and trusted. It's not the right for staff to do whatever they want. As part of the equation, staff must own the problems. Staff can only own problems when given the power to do so. Empowered staff identify and eliminate barriers to what customers need. And it's important to remember that customers don't like cumbersome processes, but they delight in the simple and easy.

Caring for library staff results in customer care. Frequent any business with happy staff, and you'll immediately know they are well cared for. Herb Kelleher, Southwest Airlines founder, built the airline's success around hiring warm, caring employees: "Employees come first and if employees are treated right, they treat the outside world right."[15] Kelleher credits Southwest Airlines employees for earning the airline the best customer-satisfaction record of any airline in America.[16] The idea behind the "Spirit of Southwest Airlines" campaign was to let potential customers know that the employees were the best: "You're telling all your prospective customers: Our People are the best. They're warm. They're hospitable. They're happy to see you. They want to help you."[17] Southwest Airlines treats staff well, empowers them to make independent decisions in favor of the customer, and expects employees to exceed customer expectations every day.

It's okay to relax procedures to eliminate obstacles that block access to products or services—go ahead and extend computer time whenever possible, waive fines, extend borrowing time, or negotiate to arrive at a "yes" transaction.[18] If we know that "yes" equals happy customers, let's stop saying "no." It blocks essential library services and drives customers away toward easier and more efficient products and services.

Staffing the service desk with rested, energetic staff who can focus on responding to customers' needs, without extra on-desk tasks, will improve your customers' library experiences.[19] Providing staff with customer service training on how to manage a variety of difficult situations and people and how to provide inclusive library services, such as addressing staff attitude toward people who are different, whether physically, intellectually, culturally, or socioeconomically, develops "yes" experiences. Giving staff the go-ahead to seek solutions for the customer without fear of repercussions will expand the library's ability to provide a legacy of library service.[20]

NOTES

1. Dave Gray and Thomas Vander Wal, *The Connected Company* (Sebastopol, CA: O'Reilly, 2012), 34.

2. Ibid.

3. Ibid.

4. John Brandon, "9 Very Specific Rules from Real Libraries," *Mental Floss*, February 10, 2013, http://mentalfloss.com/article/48843/.

5. Diane Tope Smith, comment on April 3, 2015, in response to Kathy Middleton, "Big Impact Personal Library Service," *Public Libraries Online*, February 18, 2014, http://publiclibrariesonline.org/2014/02/big-impact-personal-library-service/.

6. Library Insiders, "Contra Costa County Library Accessibility Guide," http://guides.ccclib.org/c.php?g=43933&p=277522.

7. Gray and Vander Wal, *Connected Company*, 9.

8. Ibid.

9. Bill S., comment on Yelp, September 14, 2015, https://www.yelp.com/biz/sherman-oaks-branch-library-sherman-oaks.

10. Tanya L., comment on Yelp, April 22, 2015, https://www.yelp.com/biz/baldwin-public-library-birmingham.

11. Meriden (CT) Public Library, "Customer Service Policy," http://meridenlibrary.org/wp-content/uploads/2012/12/Customer-Service-Policy.pdf (accessed November 11, 2015).

12. Boise Public Library, "Strategic Plan, Access to Library Services," www.boisepubliclibrary.org/media/4306/Mission_Vision2012-2013.pdf.

13. Lawrence (KS) Public Library, "Statement of Operating Values," http://www.lawrence.lib.ks.us/mission-statement/.

14. Monroe County (IN) Public Library, "Customer Service Policy," http://mcpl.info/geninfo/customer-service-policy.

15. Shep Hyken, *The Amazement Revolution* (Austin, TX: Greenleaf, 2011), 167.

16. John A. Byrne, *World Changers* (New York: Penguin Group, 2011), 78.

17. Ibid., 79.

18. Kathy Middleton, "The Answer Is Yes," *Public Libraries* 54, no. 1 (January/February 2015): 12.

19. Ibid.

20. Ibid.

6

Personalize Customer Service

Library customers should occupy the center of the library universe. Service should revolve around their needs and offer flexibility in a spontaneous way. At Columbus Metropolitan Library (CML), customers take center stage within the universe of the organization.[1] A dartboard-looking chart replaces compartmentalized boxes with concentric layers. The chart focuses on the customer and promotes organizational participation. Radiating from the center are the departments that support services to customers. In most organizations, the chart starts at the top and lists supporting departments below. At CML, boxes and borders are replaced with fluidity and flexibility. Closest to the customer are the services and plans that directly impact the library users, and the diagram radiates out to the four major divisions of the organization: finance, operations, customer experiences, and executive leadership. The CML Board of Trustees, Friends of the Library, and CML Foundation occupy the outermost circle and frame the entire organization. The chart is a brilliant way to remind all stakeholders that library activities revolve around customers. Communities are always changing, and so are their options for selecting products and services. Customers will always want the type of exceptional, personalized service that makes them feel cared for. A customer-focused library will recognize what its customers care about and will build its strategies around their needs.

Customers will gravitate to libraries that provide exceptional and personalized service for the simple reason that customers want to enjoy their buying (or borrowing) experience. A 2010 "Customer Experience Impact Report" found that 40 percent of people will switch to businesses that have a great reputation for customer service; 55 percent will recommend a company for its great service, not for its product or price; and 66 percent of customers report that customer service drives greater spending.[2] In short, customer service excellence will bring in new customers and retain existing customers. With so many choices of materials and resources, libraries must be committed to providing personalized service to ensure that customers return and share their experiences with others, and to attract new library users as well. Library staff are already uniquely suited to provide customized answers to both simple and complex questions, so personalizing the transaction by being attentive can only expand service possibilities.

HOW IT MAKES YOU FEEL

Personalized service is about how it makes customers feel. Think about the best customer service you've ever experienced. During those memorable transactions, the customer feels understood, important, cared for, and that someone listened and understood. Starbucks, for example, bases its success on personal connections made by employees. Rather than doing what a robot could do, employees read customers' body language, listen to their comments, use humor, and make their visits memorable. Stories about meaningful friendships between customers and employees are documented in Michelli's *The Starbucks Experience*, which points to genuine care shown by employees. Both customers and employees find meaning in some of the most ordinary moments. Howard Schultz, chairman and chief executive officer of Starbucks, in an interview with *Know*, describes the connection in this way: "The equity of the Starbucks brand is the humanity and intimacy of what goes on in the communities. . . . We continually are reminded of the powerful need and desire for human contact and for community, which is a new powerful force in determining consumer choices. . . . The Starbucks environment has become as important as the coffee itself."[3] Starbucks staff are encouraged to be themselves; bend the rules when needed; and go out of their way to make every transaction personal by looking at customers, listening to their comments, and even learning customers' names. Starbucks leadership understands that customers are people living in their community, so finding ways to connect with the community is the most authentic aspect of their service. Likewise, libraries can connect with the community outside library doors by making connections with those who come inside through the front doors, or virtually. How do we welcome those from our community into our library?

Southwest Airline's founder Herb Kelleher believed the care he showed his employees would extend to the customers.[4] The legacy Kelleher left continues today because he fostered a culture of service in which a form of the Golden Rule was followed: "Treat your employees the way you'd want them to treat customers—maybe even better."[5] The culture that Kelleher started in 1971 continues today, long after he stepped down as chairman of the board in 2008. Southwest continues to have a reputation for treating its customers well, along with the employees, who repeatedly rate the airline highly. Happy staff produce happier customers, besides creating a positive environment. Libraries can also adopt the "Employee Golden Rule" as an anchor for daily interactions in the library: treat staff the way you want them to treat customers.

The personal connection secret that makes Zappos so great is embodied in the company culture. It's known within the company as PEC (personal emotional connection).[6] Zappos encourages employees to use their own judgment and to be themselves; to allow their personalities to shine through to each customer and through the end of the transaction.[7] Zappos does not measure call times on customer service phone calls and is only concerned with going above and beyond for every customer. Giving the customer all the time he or she needs not only puts the customer in the center of the transaction but also gives staff more time to customize transactions without the pressure of a ticking clock.

Because Zappos receives thousands and thousands of phone calls and e-mails every day, opportunities abound for building the Zappos brand into the best customer service and the best customer experience.[8] The customer service focus begins after the company has made the sale. Loyal and repeat customers may get surprise upgrades to overnight shipping when they select the free shipping option.[9] Preferring to lose a sale rather than a loyal customer, Zappos will research three competitors in order to help a customer find shoes it doesn't carry. The goal is building a lifelong relationship with each customer, which may not always end in a sale, but will end with a loyal customer.

THE "WHO" IN PERSONALIZED SERVICE

Built on the premise that staff are now empowered to make decisions without fear of reprisal, examples of what personalized service represents and how it is different from traditional customer service are described here. Service, like any custom order, benefits from specifications. What do our customers care about? Customers expect customization for just about everything: food orders, home décor, vehicles, retail delivery, and online retail services. Personalized customer service changes the customer's perception of service from standard to outstanding, exceeding all expectations. Receiving customized service will surprise and amaze library customers. In the library, customization begins with listening to the customer's request, followed by "Yes, we can make that happen." *Yes! on Demand* turns standard customer service into something extraordinary for today's expectant customer.

Leaders at Zappos, Starbucks, Disney, Nordstrom, Apple, Amazon, and Ritz-Carlton value staff who will represent their products and services to a diverse audience in a personal way. Steve Jobs interviewed more than five thousand people for Apple, so he must have considered hiring the right people high on his list. He always asked, "Why are you here?"[10] If the library interviewee only wants to "be around books," or "work in a quiet environment," or isn't excited about helping customers, beware. Hiring people with the right qualifications for, but the wrong attitude about, the job is something corporate leaders and specifically the CEO of the digital marketing agency Big Spaceship warn against doing: "Don't hire jerks, no matter how talented."[11] Perhaps libraries should also adopt the "No Jerks Rule." Even in the area of technical skill, it's crucial to hire for customer service. "Attitude, rather than technical skills, is what's most important in a prospective employee. . . . You can teach technical skills,"[12] Solomon writes. Because customer service–oriented people thrive on making customers happy and are energized by helping people, library leadership should ensure they are brought on board with the values and beliefs of the library.

Because staff are so receptive during their first days on the job, customer service training should occur very early in the orientation and training period. Previous chapters discussed selecting the right people to join the library culture. Hiring for attitude is much more important than hiring for skills. Bell and Patterson, in *Customer Loyalty Guaranteed*, explain it this way: "Customer-centric organizations know that technical skills can be taught, but a desire to serve others, a willingness to engage in repeated customer contact, and a capacity to stay calm when customers lose control are often inbred attributes that must be hired for."[13] Looking for people with an aptitude for service, regardless of the position they hold in the library, will result in a fleet of service-minded staff committed to personalizing transactions in creative and caring ways.

For staff new to libraries, training should begin by describing the mission, vision, goals, and purpose of the public library, and why philosophically the customer occupies the center spot. Include in new staff orientations a welcome by library leadership that describes the library's vision. Include a library tour of internal departments and tie it in with staff's role in making customer connections. Focus on the core principles of library service in your community and provide hands-on training with yes-focused trainers, after the library's customer-centric philosophy is shared.

Shaw and Ivens, in *Building Great Customer Experiences*, describe a customer-centric company as the "outside in" approach.[14] Building systems and processes around the customer experience will result in such an "outside in" approach, which focuses on what's good for the customer. Two of seven philosophies for great customer experiences espoused by Shaw and Ivens are "enabled through inspirational leadership, an empowering culture and empathetic people who are happy and fulfilled,"[15] and "created by consistently exceeding customers' physical and emotional expectations."[16]

BE REAL

Emotional expectations can be met by using the empathetic approach with customers. Do not undervalue the potential of empathy to enhance personalized service. Empathy will serve staff well! Use it and be amazed at the happiness you will create and the number of negative transactions that will be avoided. Each of us has a natural ability to be caring and empathetic. Library products and services can only get into the hands of customers when staff commit to personalized service for each transaction. Empathy is essential to share another person's feelings. If the customer at the service desk casually states, "I haven't been inside a library for a long time," that should trigger a response aimed at welcoming him or her as a new customer. Beneath the comment may be embarrassment over not knowing how to find what's needed. A personalized response includes positive statements that reinforce the customer choice about deciding to visit the library: "Well, I'm glad you decided to come in. You're here now and that's what counts. What can I help you find today?" That is an example of personalized, caring service. There are any number of responses that communicate to the customer that you understand what he or she is experiencing, and each staff member will have a unique way of welcoming people.

In order for staff to deliver personalized customer service in ways that have made the Ritz-Carlton famous, consider the following: "The highest level of customer care is attained when service transcends attention to detail and embraces genuine empathy" and "asking questions and showing concern for your customers is valuable only if you act on those needs."[17] Empathetic responses will produce personalized results and will allow library staff to deliver customized service according to each person's preference or need.

Mercedes-Benz's employee training involves the following instruction: "Listen, Empathize, Add value and Delight" (LEAD). The immersion experience at Mercedes-Benz consists of orienting employees to the car brand and history at the maker's museum, tours of the manufacturing plant, and classroom sessions that describe both the processes and the efforts that result in an experience "Driven to Delight."[18] One of the three customer service training modules is devoted to listening and empathizing: "This module offers an opportunity to enhance your ability to listen effectively for understanding and emotionally place yourself in the position of your customer before offering solutions."[19] The successes of business giants have in common a personalized customer approach to service that relies heavily on staff ability to empathize. Create empathy scenarios for training. Staff will be responsible for making both empathetic and insensitive replies. As a result of role playing this exercise, new staff members learn why empathy is more effective than inconsiderate behavior. The extent to which personalized customer service is delivered in your library depends on the degree of customer service your staff are willing to deliver.

Empowering staff requires leaders to let go of control. The CEO of Hain Celestial Group, Irwin D. Simon, expressed it like this: "I am somebody who has learned throughout my career about empowering people, about how I don't have to be in control. . . . It's not about having an ego out there.

We all have egos, but don't let ego get in the way."[20] Staff empowerment can be liberating for some and terrifying for others, because black-and-white rules provide comfort for those who have difficulty taking chances. It is those staff members who are comfortable with the gray areas in decision making that Nordstrom seeks to hire. Their only rule, "Use good judgment in all situations,"[21] is built on the trust the employer has in its staff. For many library staff members, being trusted to make decisions in the customer's favor results in a new freedom that no longer restricts the customer. As one Nordstrom employee said: "Because we don't have many rules, we don't have to worry about breaking them. . . . We're judged on our performance, not our obedience to orders."[22] For some, the thought of only having one rule is frightening, because it's a new concept. Nordstrom's employees are judged on performance alone, not on how many rules they may have bent or obeyed. Staff enjoy their freedom at Nordstrom. Likewise, the Vanguard Group, an investment management company with $1.6 trillion in assets, inverts the traditional concept of control to the customer service representative to own the customer's issue.[23] While the customer service rep takes ownership of the customer's concern, the rest of the company acts as a support network to ensure the customer's problem is solved at the first point of service. Similarly, library supervisors can put the ownership of solving problems into staff hands to solve at the first point of service by offering them the autonomy to do so.

LET GO OF CONTROL

The Ritz-Carlton trains its staff to make independent decisions by creating the "sandbox and general rules" of playing in order for them to provide that unique and memorable interaction with guests.[24] Outcomes like those the Ritz-Carlton is seeking to achieve cannot be accomplished by micromanaged staff; control restricts creativity and squashes innovative thinking. A nineteen-year veteran of the Ritz-Carlton explains that his creativity grows from the freedom to personalize the guest experience: "Leadership exercises the patience and respect to step back and let my colleagues find their own ways to offer guests a memorable experience, just as leaders have encouraged me to create my own memorable ways."[25] When leadership trusts staff to do what's best, library staff will grow and work better together in an environment of trust. A team of empowered staff is indeed mighty!

Library staff want to be part of the mission and direction of the library. They want to take part in making decisions that affect their work environment and the customers they serve. Because of that, staff should be included in plans that affect customer service—they want to be involved in the direction and goals of the library. Staff input is also valuable for gaining a broader viewpoint. It creates staff ownership in the process and prepares future leaders. When leaders trust, empower, and include staff, their commitment deepens. In contrast, staff do not want to feel so tightly controlled that they have no voice. They want to be involved. New freedom needs to be bolstered with allowances for failure and a few guidelines:

1. **Allow failure.** Failure is an opportunity for learning. Eliminate fear before it happens by proclaiming to staff that they will not be penalized for erring on the side of the customer. Staff will become more passionate about claiming their own style of personalized customer service, and their actions will be more closely aligned with the mission of the library. Staff will thrive serving in a library in which leadership models kindness and respect and positivity. Recognizing staff by thanking them in a variety of ways—in a conversation, in written note, or in an award for going above and beyond expectations—communicates the level of appreciation staff want and deserve.

2. **Provide guidelines.** Staff want to be treated as unique, and so do customers. Both have heard "no" too many times. Provide guidelines as a starting place for staff to launch their own style of customer service using their own strengths. It will take a little time for staff to become comfortable with their freedom, but give it time, patience, and support. Provide staff with hope and encouragement by allowing a "no-guilt" structure. Mistakes should be celebrated as a learning opportunity; then it's time to move on.

When negative responses appear on social media pages or Yelp, see that as an opportunity. A customer who speaks up can be reached, whereas a customer who doesn't speak up is both dissatisfied and unreachable. Responding to complaints on social media and expanding the dialogue with a broader community proves that the library wants to listen to and solve issues. If social media complaints are left unanswered, the public will be left with the wrong impression. Addressing complaints illustrates the type of transparency that today's customer expects, and when customers read a response that personalizes the solution, they will be attracted to the message.

How would you respond if the following statement was posted on Yelp about your library? "Don't go to this library unless you want to see a bunch of homeless people smoking weed and drinking beer." You could adopt one of the following responses: (1) "Yelp is stupid, therefore I won't respond"; (2) "I don't want to touch this comment publicly—I'd rather pretend it doesn't exist"; (3) "If I answer this, I will be stooping to their level"; (4) "If I answer this, it may provoke an online argument and even more negativity"; or (5) answer the comment with, "Be assured that the library does not tolerate illegal activity and we want to make certain everyone has a great library experience. We care about our community just as much as you do, so please report any illegal activity to the library and/or law enforcement." If the library does not respond to the comment, readers may think it is true, or others will add to the comments, and the antilibrary thread will grow. It just makes sense to set the record straight. By acknowledging the problem, customers will understand the library is engaged in the community.

Librarians are notorious for using jargon, and jargon can kill communication when used with library customers. Library acronyms are particularly annoying for customers to try to decipher, and many really don't care to learn them. What do the terms "Claims Return," "circulation," or "ILS" mean to customers? What do the terms: "audiovisual," "serial," "OPAC," "database," "periodical," "stacks," or "juvenile fiction" actually mean to people? Try describing jargony terms in the vernacular:

Claims return: "No worries. We'll take that book off your account."
OPAC: "Let's go take a look at what's available in stock."
Database: "We have online articles and books also."
Serial: "We have magazines and newspapers, or you can download digital copies to your phone or tablet."
Juvenile fiction: "The kids' books are over here."
Audiovisual materials: "We have movies; this way."
Readers' advisory: "I'd love to find a good book for you."

Talking with customers in understandable terms provides a personal touch that will help build a connection with them. Ford, McNair, and Perry (2009) suggest matching the customer's speed and style as well as matching his or her emotion.[26] There's merit to that philosophy, especially because public library staff communicate with people of all ages and backgrounds. They suggest that if a person speaks slowly, slow down your own speech; if a person has a limited vocabulary, reduce your own vocabulary to simple words; and if a person speaks particularly fast, step up your own response a bit. Aligning their responses to the degree of emotional intensity of the customer suggests that staff have empathy, which goes a long way toward easing a customer's concerns. "If the customer is natural, you are natural. If the customer is angry, show concern. If the customer is in a panic, show a sense of urgency. If the customer is friendly, you are cheerful. . . . If the customer is frustrated, you are empathetic."[27] Empathy without action may not provide what the customer seeks.

PROVIDE CHOICES

Personalized customer service also includes being able to offer customers a variety of choices—digital resources or lucky day collections, for example—for library services that reflect customers' requests. Services such as library hours can reflect the personal needs of the community in which the library resides. Surveying customers to learn what library hours would best fit their lives can inform decisions for changing open hours or days of the week, without the need to increase the number of open hours. Likewise, customers can be surveyed on program types and time schedules in order to personalize their requests. If evening storytimes fit your customers' needs, juggle desk schedules and switch to providing pajama storytimes.

CHALLENGING INTERACTIONS

So far this discussion has addressed ways to say "yes" more with customization and active listening. But what if the customer is leaving a nasty review about your library on Yelp? What if the customer approaching you is already very upset? Sometimes customization means de-escalating and mediating with angry customers. Most customer service experts agree that customers get angry for the following reasons: "Expectations are not met; someone was rude; someone was indifferent, or no one listened."[28] In the context of library service, how often do customers expect the library to be quiet and serene, and that just isn't the case? Library visitors today don't learn and enjoy the library in a mausoleum-like environment, nor do they communicate in whispers. Library staff should make sure customers don't go overboard on noisiness, but normal tones are preferred to whispering these days. Library staff can suggest a study room, quiet zone, or earphones, and explain that the library is busy with activity, which generates noise, and what a great problem to have—a busy, vibrant library! Keeping the conversation positive, being confident in your message about the library—for example, sharing how many children are reading at higher levels; how many parents are learning early literacy skills; or how many teens are finding a place to have face-to-face time with friends, study, do homework, or use the computers—shows the customer that the mission of the library is being accomplished, and you will try to accommodate his or her unique needs as best you can.

Rudeness—ah, rudeness. Rude staff bring out anger (or at least irritation) in about everyone. Rude behavior blocks customer service and drives customers away from the library. Embarrassing, insulting, and humiliating customers has no place in public service. Neither does sarcasm. Customers who start conversations with rude behavior should be met with courtesy, and if you feel as if you're about to blow a cork over a rude customer, call for backup. None of us is exempt from experiencing or reacting to rude or insensitive treatment. Do what you can to de-escalate the offensive behavior, and after you've tried using empathy, good listening skills, and a positive demeanor, but nothing is working, consider yourself empowered to bring any verbal abuse to an end by firmly asking the customer to leave the library.

Indifference is the robotic behavior that suggests a library staff member does not care at all. You might hear phrases such as, "That's against policy," "They won't let us do that," or "I don't know." Each of those responses suggests that staff are not supported to make decisions, aren't on board with library goals, or are not working in support of a collaborative team. Make customer service a priority. Share the mission and vision of the library with staff so they embrace a "we" attitude rather than a "they" attitude. Failing to listen to the customer also brings out angst in the customer. It demonstrates that staff do not care and don't want to expend the energy to solve the problem or listen to the concern. When staff shut down a customer concern, the problem will not go away; in fact, it will escalate. We must decide at the onset of the transaction that we are dedicated to finding a customized solution to the request based on the question. We should reach into our library toolbox of resources to pull out whatever is needed to satisfy the customer request. That is how we will establish lifelong customers and lifelong learners for the next generation of library users.

Did you know that 93 percent of any message is communicated not through words but through tone of voice and physical presence (body language)?[29] That's an astounding fact to consider for delivering personal customer service. The customer transaction is either doomed or enhanced by how the customer perceives our level of service. Tone of voice will also influence how a customer responds to service. So it really doesn't matter what words are contained in the greeting for all staff to use; what matters is the tone and way in which it's conveyed. A friendly demeanor and tone provide the best stage possible for library staff to do their magic and connect people with all of the greatness in the library universe.

In the journey to provide service based on what the customer needs, whether communicated by tone, body language, or words, remember to listen carefully before responding. Do not interrupt, finish a person's sentence, or start guessing what he or she might want before listening completely; wait until the customer is finished talking before you speak. Repeat to the customer what you heard and confirm that you understood him or her correctly. Even if you've been asked a similar question in the past, be patient and pay attention to clues that will allow you to provide outstanding advice and service. This could be a great opportunity to practice or explore new ways to personalize the request and connect with the customer.

Simply listening or "hearing someone out" is not the same as caring. Maintain eye contact with the customer and try not to be distracted by coworkers, work, or other things on your mind. If you are not focusing on the customer, you will lose an opportunity to develop a lifelong customer. You cannot actively listen if you are formulating your argument for "no." Focus on the present conversation and remember that the customer is your highest priority at that moment. While engaged in active listening, imagine how you will solve the customer's concern with a particular product or service that will satisfy the request and result in a positive, "yes" library experience.

Assisting customers at their point of need on demand will produce positive customer experiences, which is what public libraries should strive to do. Scheduling appointments for customers to return does not satisfy the immediate need of many customers. If library leadership embraces the concept that personalized customer service is the key to continuing the library's sustainability into the future, then they should encourage staffing flexibility and focus on that end. Scheduling backup staff to abandon backroom processes in favor of attending to the customer will ultimately result in gaining a life customer and a few good referrals! Loyal, happy customers will share their experiences with friends, family, or colleagues; they might submit online feedback that benefits the library's position in the community. It's time to think of the customer as occupying the highest level of our library culture. Processes that take place in the library workroom take second place in a culture of personalized customer service. Lengthier customer transactions can be supported by summoning staff from other areas to assist. To develop a culture of service, staff must be eager to assist customers who require extra help and see this as an opportunity to practice *Yes! on Demand*.

EXTRAORDINARY PERSONALIZED SERVICE

What are the ways library staff can make the customer experience personal? A story about Ace Hardware Corporation in *The Amazement Revolution* illustrates one of the most extreme forms of customer service described any-where. An elderly woman visiting an Ace hardware store in Florida was look-ing at Christmas trees and remarked that she'd love to have the tree she was admiring, but it was too tall for her to decorate at her age. The woman was not seeking a solution to her situation, and she was surprised when the manager, who had overheard her, said that he'd not only deliver the tree, but help her decorate it. What resulted was a nine-year tradition of tree decorating and eating banana bread at the elderly woman's home each holiday season. The store manager became part of her life. When she passed away, the manager was among the ten people at her funeral. She'd shared her story with her neigh-bors, many of whom came to shop at the store after hearing her story. This is an extreme example of personalized service, but the concept is valid for librar-ies. The manager listened to the elderly woman's comment, offered a personal-ized solution, developed a longtime friendship, and created goodwill in the community. Library employees can create similar stories to share with the community.

RECOGNIZING THE NEED

The reference interview provides a good example of a personalized service transaction. We listen, ask clarifying questions, provide an answer, and fol-low up to see if the information need was met. It is really that simple. How? Based on the American Library Association's Reference and User Services Association (RUSA) reference interview, listen, then go one or two steps further: connect customers with additional products and services, form rela-tionships with customers so it's less about a single person's need and more about meeting people's overall needs.

Yes! on Demand begins with staff understanding how to use library products and services and how to promote them. If a customer wants to check out a book that is not on the shelf, the ensuing transaction should seamlessly provide alternatives based on product knowledge. Staff should be comfortable with technologies that connect people to digital titles and databases. Staff must be proficient in proposing alternatives to resources that are unavailable in order to provide service that exceeds customer requests. Customers should not leave the library unsatisfied or unhappy due to "no" responses. When staff are skilled in technology and can seamlessly help customers with questions about digital resources, smartphones, tablets, e-readers, or social media, customers will recognize the validation of their questions and the immediacy with which a solution is provided. Staff should be aware of the many services, programs, and opportunities the library offers in order to share relevant resources with the customer.

Personalize Library Service

- Place customer needs in the center of the library universe.
- Hire the right people, those who have the capacity to connect with people and who possess product knowledge, listening skills, and empathy.
- Recognize that staff are the most important resource in the library.
- Trust staff, surrender control over transactions, and empower staff to create customer happiness.
- Use empowerment to make decisions in the customer's favor; stay current on library products and services to offer the best solutions.
- Contribute to the culture: *Yes! on Demand* service is a result of all staff being dedicated to serving each other and the public.

This chapter has discussed the importance of a customer-centric library and how to create a library experience in which the customer feels important, listened to, and cared for, in which his or her options are customized. It provided some real-life examples, for both leadership and frontline staff, of how to offer personalized and customized customer service to our community, gain new customers, and keep our current visitors. To create a customer-centric library, we all really need to step up our customer service game. It starts with saying "yes" more and hiring "yes" people. Immerse staff in customer service training and empower them to be themselves and to make mistakes when they are acting in favor of the customer. Allow staff to work autonomously and have a stake in the library. It is important to make a connection with your customers, even those who may be difficult to understand. Be knowledgeable about the library's products and services and explore your own ways to say "yes" to customers.

NOTES

1. Columbus Metropolitan Library, "CMS Organization Chart," http://www .columbuslibrary.org/organization-chart.

2. Gary Vaynerchuk, *The Thank You Economy* (New York: HarperCollins, 2011), 87.

3. Joseph A. Michelli, *The Starbucks Experience* (New York: McGraw-Hill, 2007), 28.

4. Shep Hyken, *The Amazement Revolution* (Austin, TX: Greenleaf, 2011), 167.

5. Ibid., 167–168.

6. Tony Hsieh, *Delivering Happiness* (New York: Business Plus, 2010), 145.

7. Ibid.

8. Ibid., 144.

9. Ibid.

10. John A. Byrne, *World Changers* (New York: Penguin Group, 2011), 91.

11. Adam Bryant, *Quick and Nimble* (New York: Henry Holt, 2014), 70–71.

12. Micah Solomon, *High-Tech, High-Touch Customer Service* (New York: AMACOM, 2012), 86.

13. Chip R. Bell and John R. Patterson, *Customer Loyalty Guaranteed* (Avon, MA: Adams Business, 2007), 212.

14. Colin Shaw and John Ivens, *Building Great Customer Experiences* (New York: Palgrave Macmillan, 2002), 8.

15. Ibid., 9.

16. Ibid.

17. Joseph A. Michelli, *The New Gold Standard: 5 Leadership Principles for Creating a Legendary Customer Experience Courtesy of The Ritz-Carlton Hotel Company* (New York: McGraw Hill, 2008), 161.

18. Joseph Michelli, *Driven to Delight* (New York: McGraw-Hill Education, 2016) 142–143.

19. Ibid., 144.

20. Adam Bryant, *Quick and Nimble* (New York: Henry Holt, 2014), 64.

21. Robert Spector and Patrick McCarthy, *The Nordstrom Way* (Hoboken, NJ: John Wiley & Sons, 2005), 143.

22. Ibid.

23. Dave Gray and Thomas Vander Wal, *The Connected Company* (Sebastopol, CA: O'Reilly, 2012), 37.

24. Michelli, *New Gold Standard*, 109.

25. Ibid.

26. Lisa Ford, David McNair, and William Perry, *Exceptional Customer Service*, 2nd ed. (Avon, MA: Adams Business, 2009), 106.

27. Ibid.

28. Ibid., 134.

29. Ibid., 103.

7

Break and Fix Rules

We've discussed *Yes! on Demand* guidelines for leaders, frontline staff, and customers, and learned why "no" attitudes and actions sabotage service. Today's customers expect and demand personalized service from business— service that makes life enjoyable. Businesses that provide personalized service delivered by empowered employees lead in profits and win over their competitors. Eliminating "no" and getting to "yes" is the new standard for customer service, and libraries can join in. Getting to *Yes! on Demand* requires reviewing library policies and procedures, specifically ones that are viewed as draconian and irrational in today's culture. Changing no-focused policies requires a library infrastructure built for the customer, around which revolve library products and services. A customer-centric focus anchors justification for policy realignment.

An organization's culture, values, and basic guidelines are far more important than its rules. The library has the potential to change lives in its community. If employees embrace the library's culture and values, it follows that they will modify their actions to provide service. Top businesses unabashedly proclaim the company's specific values and are excited to share these values. For instance, employees at Amazon know exactly what the company stands for, so taking action is clear. "They don't need to check with anybody, because they know what Amazon stands for. So they can simply act."[1]

Library leadership and staff are familiar with rules, procedures, and policy that direct customer service transactions. Staff are expected to understand library rules in order to tell customers what is or is not allowed. Procedures based in policy ensure that specific actions are performed in a particular way, every possible scenario cannot be planned to fit within policy guidelines. Policy should provide the general goals of the library's governing body. The Middle French origin of the word "policy" is "policier," or "police"—to control, regulate, and keep in order.[2] The word "policy" is rooted in enforcement, guarding, and protecting. Quoting policy to customers essentially puts staff in the position of policing library resources. It's no surprise that customers bristle at the sound of it.

RULES

Library rules were designed to ensure fairness in access to products and services mutually owned by a community of participating citizens. Basic rules should provide consistency. Staff feel safe relying on them for direction. Public library rules have changed over the past one-hundred-plus years but have not progressed beyond expectations for proper use of materials borrowed. In the public library's early beginnings, rules provided visitors with expectations about their behavior while they visited the library. The public was instructed in the proper handling of books and how to treat them gently. The concept of a free library had never before existed, and the public immediately gained access to a universe of learning. Over the years, rules were still centered on protecting library assets, customer behavior, and the consequences of infractions. Indeed, library rules keep people safe, protect library resources, and protect a customer's First Amendment right to enjoy the library. But rules, policies, and procedures should be reviewed regularly in order to reflect relevance in a changing community. In the name of consistency, strict rules often prevent staff from exercising freedom to problem solve using their own good judgment on a case-by-case basis. When faced with the dilemma of giving the customer what he or she wants versus what the rules dictate, staff may feel more comfortable strictly adhering to rules. Rules provide security when staff are faced with decision making. Staff may fear repercussions from supervisors. Declining a customer's request is certainly not the best outcome for the customer, but staff will want to protect their career interests in favor of erring on the customer's side.

When a particular policy, rule, or procedure consistently produces an outcry from customers, it's time for review and a new direction for a new customer paradigm. Outdated policies reflect a culture and customer of the past. Culture changes and library rules should reflect it; the only constant to fall back on is change. Enforcing a rule that no longer makes sense places staff in the position of defending arcane procedures that end in conflict. It's not heresy to suggest library policies receive regular scrutiny and refinement; successful businesses routinely review policies for relevance and rely on employees to identify flaws. Employees at Zappos, Amazon, and Starbucks bend rules by personalizing orders and doing whatever is necessary to make customers happy and exceed expectations. Business, retail, and service industries limit rules to keep it simple. The problem with procedures are, as Gray and Vander Wal suggest, that they are designed to "predictably and reliably solve any problem that should arise."[3] But because the processes in any organization are apt to break down, fixes are often made by adding even more rules to handle exceptions.[4] Procedures and rules ensure that frontline employees are not faced with making decisions, which is not a good practice, as discussed by Gray and Vander Wal, "and the more problems and solutions we define in advance, the more difficult it becomes for employees to understand or even find the rules that apply in a given situation."[5] Not every customer problem can be identified in advance in rules. Customer-focused businesses such as Zappos, Starbucks, and Amazon adopt employee empowerment as a means to deliver personalized and yes-focused customer solutions. Each of these winning businesses trusts the employee to use good judgment in the best interests of the customer and the business. With that in mind, rules become simply baggage that impedes customer satisfaction.

Staff must be given a voice in identifying policies and procedures entrenched in "no." Jeanne Bliss, in *Chief Customer Officer 2.0*, describes "killing stupid rules" that get in the way of employees delivering value: "These rules frustrate customers and employees. . . . These rules frustrate employees who repeatedly bring them up to leaders, without seeing them removed. Your employees are put in the position of having to defend practices and rules that they don't agree with, and over time that impacts their belief in the values of the organization and its belief in them."[6] Punitive and outdated rules obstruct business growth and take away any competitive edge. Libraries can learn from businesses that review policies on a yearly basis and have purged senseless rules. Library staff on the front lines will be happy to provide examples of stupid rules when asked and can identify solutions to outdated policies.

Dan Pastoric, executive vice president and chief customer officer for Enersource, reviews company policies to ensure rules and procedures are up to date with "changing technology, business philosophies, and customer trends."[7] By asking "Does this policy still fit with our changing culture?," Enersource can eliminate unnecessary procedures in favor of getting something done.[8] Pastoric asks his employees to make decisions based on how they would treat their mom, in order to treat customers in a more connected and human way.[9] In the end, transactions must be centered on humanizing the customer experience.

Everyone in the library needs a voice in identifying rules that obstruct customer service. If library staff hear the same complaints from customers over and over, it's time to review and change the rules. For example, if library policy requires that the library dispose of lost or damaged materials, even if the patron pays for the item, expect to hear complaints. Even though the customer may not be paying for the explicit item in hand, a customer will not want to be told that he or she cannot keep the damaged item. In a retail situation, a customer who breaks an item can take it home after paying for it. The same should apply to libraries. Rigid library rules drive customers away and are the antithesis of yes-focused customer service. Policy change is unique for each library, but it must be centered in this precept: err on the side of customer access. Change irrelevant rules that block *Yes! on Demand*. Solicit feedback from frontline staff to identify rules that irritate and drive customers away.

Rules and policies are frustrating for customers. In retail situations, customers expect service based on their needs, not the needs of the business. Library policies and rules often block customers from the products and services they request. Fines and other hindrances to borrowing, from a customer perspective, translate into negative customer service. If we are willing to write into procedures variances in policy in order to further the mission, and to equip staff to recognize when, for example, to waive or reduce fines, customers will be more likely to connect with the library for a repeat experience.

Many angry patron encounters begin with notification of fines, lost book fees, and similar notifications by staff, which the patron sees as contradictory to the concept of the public library and at odds with customer service standards. Changes that require decisions in policy and require approval by library governance can be accomplished over time and if they are based on the library's strategic direction, but in the meantime, listen to customers, offer alternatives, and seek to solve problems anchored in "no."

Evaluating the success of *Yes! on Demand* service requires checking in with the public through survey tools. How do communities support the library? Support can be measured through outputs such as attendance at programs, the number of materials checked out, or voter response on a tax measure. Outcome measurement will inform the ways in which the library has made a difference in a customer's behavior, attitude, or skill level. What ticks people off? Complaints originate from a variety of sources—staff attitudes, lack of materials, library hours, lack of diversity in resources and programs—along with rules that cut customers off from library products and services.

Yes! on Demand requires soft skills, learned skills, and technical skills. As discussed in previous chapters, libraries must hire people with the right attitude. Attitude is not a science; it can't be learned. Employers cannot teach people to be genuinely nice or caring or show empathy, so it's important to select the right people.

To achieve *Yes! on Demand* customer service, one must watch for nonverbal cues and listen for customer prompts that will lead to the best outcome. Empathy encourages staff to solve customer problems by putting themselves in the customer's shoes. Being aware of customer body language and making eye contact will encourage dialogue. Staff who synthesize questions and comments will develop creative options to share with the customer. By exploring options from the extensive toolbox of learned skills that librarians possess and drawing on their strengths and skills, staff will provide customers with a personal and customized response. Based on their knowledge of library products and services, staff can identify what will not only satisfy but also outshine customer expectations. Staff should expect to both give and receive happiness.

CUSTOMER SERVICE STATEMENTS

A review of customer service statements among libraries in America yielded an assortment of rules and policies. Some were very strict and foreboding, while others were pleasantly inviting. Tucked between the lines of otherwise innocuous rules, the following less-than-positive instruction was noted: "Let's trust our patrons unless the individual history of a patron has shown us they are not trustworthy." Whoops! Perhaps that could have been framed this way: "We trust our patrons and will make the best judgment possible in all transactions." Another instruction, located in a long list of borrower's card rules, stated: "Registered patrons who do not have their card with them when borrowing materials may show proof of identification. However, this privilege may not be abused. A patron who habitually 'forgets' their card will be asked to come back with the card or replace it if it is lost." Is the rule aimed at forgetful folks, after-school teens, or any person (intellectual disabilities included) who can't seem to keep his or her card in his or her pocket? How about offering suggestions for people who habitually forget their cards? If the cardholder's name is known, retrieve the card number for him or her. Suggest keeping the barcode in the customer's smartphone, or find other creative ideas that suggest empathy and support.

Interlibrary loans require a fair amount of processing and staff time. It irritates staff to devote so much time and effort to the process, only to learn that customer holds are not being picked up. This problem may be seen in the following rules, which ironically were created to fix the problem: "The ILL process is very time consuming and costly both to the [library withheld] and the staff that is kindly lending the material. To that end, the following repercussions are placed on ILLs that are not picked up or are overdue: 1) 1st time item not picked up: patron blocked from ILL for 6 months, 2) 2nd time item not picked up . . . patron blocked from ILL for 1 year; 3) 3rd time item not picked up . . . patron blocked permanently from ILL." The rule is clearly meant to reduce the number of abandoned holds, but it could be better addressed by identifying the particular customers who present egregious challenges, by making a call to those customers to address and solve the problem. Life often gets in the way of picking up holds and managing personal time.

SOCIAL MEDIA

With the rise of social media, customers have exponentially found empowerment on the Internet to both praise and bash public libraries. Potential new library customers may "yelp" a library in order to get an idea of what to expect on their visit. Customers find reviews time-saving. In addition to posting comments online, library customers want to be heard and included in the planning, discussion, and evaluation of library products and services. Micah Solomon describes "today's changed customer" as one who can bring a complaint instantly under public scrutiny via Twitter through the speed of the Internet.[10] In the past, libraries received complaints in letters, online comment forms, or e-mails. It's imperative that libraries respond to negative comments posted online rather than ignore these comments. Library customers can post comments immediately, and as Solomon asserts, "they expect you to understand it too, to incorporate the empowerment expectations of customers into your problem-resolution process. In other words, understand that the playing field has flattened—or prepare to be flattened yourself."[11] Libraries need to pay attention to negative public forum comments and reply courteously, so the potential library customer will know that his or her concerns are being addressed and customer service is at the top of the library's priority list.

Celebrate customer stories with all staff. It's important for everyone to know how the library accomplishes its mission every day. Report staff actions that change people's lives in the community—those that go beyond basic customer service—to inspire staff to make personalized customer service decisions based on what the customer needs when he or she needs it. This often includes stepping outside of normal rules that libraries have traditionally held close. Empowered staff will take these steps when library leadership support their doing so. Expect to receive feedback from those in the community touched by *Yes! on Demand.*

PUBLIC LIBRARIES CHANGE LIVES

Yes! on Demand: A Customer Story

Dear Library Director,

Please thank the staff of [unnamed] Public Library for their noteworthy, kind, and generous, helpful assistance yesterday evening. At approximately 5:55 PM yesterday, after my regular workday was completed, I had taken my personal vehicle to Library. In the library parking lot I saw a man wearing multiple layers of disheveled clothing. The man was seated in the winter's cold and darkness of night on a worn-out and old-looking three-wheel electric-motorized mobility scooter. I could quickly tell this man seated on his scooter was not doing considerably well in life. I observed how the man seated on his scooter appeared to be attempting to reconnect and/or repair wires located under his scooter's console. I asked the man on the scooter if he needed some help. The man informed me his scooter had stopped working, leaving him stranded in the parking lot. This man I met with the broken scooter also told me he was having trouble due to the cold and darkness to repair his scooter by himself, adding his broken scooter was his only means of personal transportation. (Later in the evening I would learn this man had become dependent upon his old and now-broken scooter after reportedly becoming disabled after falling 3½ stories in a construction site accident. The man with the broken scooter also remarked to me he had become hesitant in life to trust strangers, particularly after he was robbed by another man when he had become stranded on his scooter before.) As I spoke with this man stranded on his scooter in library parking lot yesterday, the man said he had no tools or even a flashlight or other materials necessary to make his needed scooter repairs; and to compound the problem of the broken scooter, the man stranded in the parking lot reported to me he was destitute, homeless, and didn't even have a cell phone. I went inside library to see if maybe I could get some adhesive tape to possibly do a temporary fix on the disabled man's scooter. Inside the library, I observed the library staff was closing things down for the day. While I may be wrong, it also appeared that all the visitors/patrons had already left the library for the day. I briefly explained to library personnel standing at the library's checkout counter the predicament of the disabled man stranded outside in the parking lot. The public library staff freely provided me some adhesive tape to reconnect and secure wires and assemblies that had broken and come loose on the man's scooter. That was not all library personnel did to help yesterday. I observed how the female library personnel remained at the library after closing time to just be of assistance if needed and to help if asked. One female librarian even offered and gave me more tape to use too. The male librarian working at the library yesterday also stayed after library closing hours as well. This male library employee even located a pair of pliers needed to help strip electrical wire on the disabled man's scooter. Thus, as far as I could tell, all of your library staff on duty stayed after official closing time to help in whatever way needed to help ensure this disabled man would not be left stranded. And it really made a difference; for example, the male Public Library employee's cell phone (or whoever library employee provided the cell phone) provided the light necessary to be able to locate and to fix the broken scooter wires—and the male librarian even helped me to find a wire that had broken loose and fallen onto the scooter's floor. And that was not all. After the disabled man's scooter was repaired (at least enough to get the owner of the scooter to where he wanted to go), we learned there was not enough electricity remaining in the scooter's batteries to adequately propel the man to his desired destination down the street. The library male staff member helped me load the partially taken-apart scooter into the back of my pickup. Later, at the gas station, I was surprised to find the male employee (and maybe other library staff) had even driven to the gas station to help me some more to assist this disabled man. Within a relatively short time last night, the man's repaired scooter was eventually hooked up to an electrical outlet at the gas station to get recharged. And while I know none of the names of these library employees—and never directly asked anyone at the library for anything more than some tape that I can recall—I am grateful your library staff exhibited noble concern, kind generosity, and even an immediate readiness and complete willingness to offer me assistance yesterday—even after I had left with the disabled man in my truck from the library. In closing, the help of library staff yesterday truly reflected more than a mere casual display of routine public service work. It was true compassion I observed as staff helped to assist in whatever way that could possibly be done at the moment to help a reportedly homeless disabled man in the community obviously struggling and suffering, and in immediate need of some assistance. And while not the most-perfect ending to a series of very unfortunate events and circumstances for this disabled man with his old scooter, at least this man with his now-repaired scooter is hopefully now afforded some return to a better level of personal mobility, and at least the opportunity to continue with his personal pursuits to a hopefully better life in the days to follow. I want you to know I am thankful to library staff for helping and exhibiting by their actions very extraordinary and commendable public service work yesterday.

Sincerely,
Clayton Nye

Mr. Nye's e-mail to the library director described the way in which he was touched by the exceptional service of library staff. Staff cared more for the customer than themselves, as they stayed after closing to offer their help. The library supervisor stepped outside of his usual role to help a person in the community; he saw the bigger need that affected a person's life in his library community. Mr. Nye not only felt compelled to write to the library, he agreed to share his story with the larger library community.

Public Libraries magazine published a poignant customer service story that described a child's perspective on a yes-focused transaction that influenced the youngster's life direction. In a public library years ago, a hardworking, single mother with two children in tow broke down in tears over the $35 fine separating her children from their Christmas presents that year—a stack of library books. The librarian responded with empathy and understanding. That librarian broke library rules and replied: "You know what, don't worry about it, take the books, Merry Christmas." That little boy grew up to be a public library director.[12]

There are many stories of exceptional public library service that far surpass any customer expectations. Stories of staff exceeding what the customer expected and what library leadership expected as well. These are the stories public libraries need to celebrate and share. Stories that build communities and the people in them. Stories that bring staff outside of library walls to meet people where they are. In tumultuous times, after fires, hurricanes, floods, and riots, dedicated public library staff rescue people who are not exactly sure where they are going or what they're looking for, but go to the public library to find help in the form of humanity and kindness, delivered by heroes on the front line.

NOTES

1. Dave Gray and Thomas Vander Wal, *The Connected Company* (Sebastopol, CA: O'Reilly, 2012), 217.

2. *Merriam-Webster*, s.v. "policy," http://www.merriam-webster.com/dictionary/policy (accessed March 5, 2016).

3. Gray and Vander Wal, *Connected Company*, 112.

4. Ibid.

5. Ibid.

6. Jeanne Bliss, *Chief Customer Officer 2.0* (Hoboken, NJ: John Wiley & Sons, 2015), 170.

7. Ibid., 171.

8. Ibid.

9. Ibid.

10. Micah Solomon, *High-Tech, High-Touch Customer Service* (New York: AMACOM, 2012), 17.

11. Ibid.

12. Peter Struzziero, "The Power of Yes," *Public Libraries* 54, no. 1 (January/February 2015): 25.

Appendix

Everything in this appendix is credited to the wonderful, fabulous Yes!
Customer Service Team, Sacramento Public Library: Amber, Bruce, Claudia,
Christopher, Christie, Harsimar, Janet, Katherine, Kristi, Molly, Raina, and
Thom.

There are people who just have a knack for providing excellent customer service. At Sacramento Public Library, a team is made up of those people—those library staff who responded to the recruitment of a new Yes! Customer Service Team. As part of the recruitment process, potential members were asked four questions:

1. *Why are you interested in joining the Yes! Team? In what ways will you contribute?*
2. *Name your favorite retailer (either online or physical location) where you most often find yourself browsing or buying. Why?*
3. *Describe a time when you (as a customer) had the best customer service experience of your life. What made it the best?*
4. *Describe a time when you thought outside the box to provide exceptional service for an SPL patron; for instance, you worked to create a positive outcome for the customer, despite a library policy, procedure, or practice that made it difficult to do so.*

When the team met for the first time, they took turns reading excerpts pulled out of an envelope taken from the applications. These were accounts of library staff and supervisors going out of their way to make sure customers were happy and had what they needed, often during complex transactions requiring multiple steps. In some instances, staff broke or bent policy. The result: the library didn't go bankrupt, and everyone lived to talk about it. Without having permission to make independent decisions outside of policy, these creative individuals erred on the side of access and used their own good judgment to bring about delightful resolutions to problems. In all one dozen team responses, we noticed some patterns:

- A need was observed by staff or requested by the customer: the connection.
- That need evoked a response to solve a problem or provide service beyond basic help: the cue or a trigger.
- A decision was made to solve the customer's problem, regardless of multiple steps or difficulty in achieving success: the commitment.
- Staff crossed the line from basic to personalized and customized service in order to provide a product or service: empowerment.
- The customer was thrilled and surprised by the extent of the service: happy customer.
- The staff person was happy to provide the service and easily recalled details of the transaction: staff fulfillment.
- Yes! Customer Service Team responses brought inspiration and encouragement and hope for staff and will bring the same to customers.

Yes-Focused Customer Service
MANIFESTO

INTRODUCTION

What Is Yes-Focused Customer Service?

Yes-focused customer service is a premier customer service model for Sacramento Public Library (SPL) staff and emulates award-winning customer service models found in top businesses. We believe that each customer is unique, and we recognize that our staff—more than books, computers, or anything else the library contains—are the most important resource in the library. Staff will astound customers with their knowledge and delivery of personalized service. Staff must be empowered to make independent decisions in favor of the customer's needs, in an environment of trust, which begins at the top. Yes-focused service guides customers through their entire transaction, without ever leaving concerns unresolved. Yes-focused staff will listen for cues that trigger thoughtful solutions and require staff to have a thorough knowledge of resources. We want our service to exceed customer expectations, to the extent that the library experiences we create are worth sharing. We want to listen to our customers' suggestions and complaints, quickly reply, and respond to their feedback. Yes-focused customer service must begin with SPL leaders and permeate every position within the organization. The customer service culture begins to develop when SPL staff at every level recognize the value of customers as the life and future of the library. Providing premier customer service changes lives. To stay competitive in today's consumer-savvy market, we must place the highest value on our staff's ability to amaze and exceed customer expectations.

Sacramento Public Library Strategic Goal 2: Develop and empower staff to create a culture of customer service that ensures positive experiences for our diverse community.

SPL Strategic Objectives

2.1 Patrons have increased confidence that they will have a respectful and yes-focused experience at the library.

2.2 Patrons have increased confidence in staff knowledge and skills to meet their service and program needs.

2.3 Patrons have increased confidence that the library and its staff reflect the diverse needs of their community.

Customer Service Goals

- To give our customers and each other unsurpassed service
- To deliver personalized, individual, and unexpected service
- To identify and remove customer obstacles
- To equip staff to deliver a yes-focused experience
- To empower staff to make independent decisions in favor of the customer
- To bring happiness to the lives of customers and staff
- To value diversity in our customers and ourselves

Creating a Culture of "Yes"

- Leadership must buy in and be the first to model a "yes" culture.
- Leadership visits branches regularly and spends time with staff.
- All staff participate.
- Staff exchange programs for cross-learning.
- Staff have a collective pride and commitment to achieving "yes."
- The customer experience is personalized by staff recognizing "ask triggers."
- Staff are encouraged to make judgment calls in favor of the customer.
- Staff review policies and procedures that block access, listen to and respond to customer complaints, and create "no" logs to find patterns or repetitive "nos." It may be time to change a policy or procedure.
  - The library may increase minimum fine levels.
  - If we know a customer's identity, and he or she arrives without a library card, why do we ask for ID? Staff must be empowered to use their own good judgment, within basic guidelines.
  - When a customer needs more computer time, staff should not ask, "Why do you need to use the computer?"
  - If a customer wants to use the phone, staff should not reply, "Whom do you want to call?"

Train New Staff

- Each customer receives personal service based on cues that prompt a custom solution.
- Clear instructions are provided and delivered by the Yes! Team.
- New staff are internal customers.
- Staff are encouraged and trusted to make judgment calls in favor of the customer.
- The Yes! Team provides customer service training for new and existing staff.

- Staff shadow the best of the best in the field.
- There is face-to-face, small-group, and/or one-on-one training.
- Videos demonstrate the ideal.
- The Danger Room shows scenarios of complex transactions.
- Staff work toward eliminating "no."
- A decompressing station is available.
- Staff receive follow-up training.
- Training is consistently delivered.
- New staff are told that customers are people, not transactions.

Train All Existing Staff

- Clear instructions are provided and delivered by the Yes! Team.
- Staff are encouraged and trusted to make judgment calls in favor of the customer.
- Each customer receives personal service based on triggers that prompt a custom solution.
- Training is delivered by the Yes! Team.
- When needed/desired, staff shadow the best of the best in the field and get follow-up training.
- There is face-to-face, small-group, and/or one-on-one training.
- Videos demonstrate the ideal.
- Training emphasizes customer service points each month at staff meetings, role-play, discussion, and strategy.
- Staff are matched with needed training.
- The Danger Room shows scenarios of complex transactions.
- Staff work toward eliminating "no."
- A decompressing station is available.
- Training is consistently delivered.
- All departments are expected to find "yes" solutions for internal and external customers.
- Supervisors are expected to lead, support, and empower staff to "own" customer service solutions.

Train Using Standards and Goals

- Identify key areas that impact staff morale, knowledge, and confidence in delivering friendly and knowledgeable customer service.
- Improve key areas that impact staff morale, knowledge, and confidence in delivering friendly and knowledgeable customer service.

- Establish standards and goals for all staff to complete.
- Provide accountability measures.
- Evaluate training competencies using a checklist.
- Evaluate performance on training.
- Provide enhanced Sierra training and policy/procedure training; shadowing the best of the best in the field, and follow-up training.
- Provide enhanced training in the new hire's specific position; shadowing the best of the best in the field, and follow-up training.

Deliver Training in a Variety of Formats

- Group activities
- Scenarios
- Three-minute videos
- Role-play
- Mentors: buddy system or cohort for new staff

Training Coordinator and Trainers

- One or two members of the Yes! Team deliver training for two or more branches.
- One or two members of the Yes! Team deliver new staff training that includes an orientation checklist with competencies.
- The Yes! Team, in coordination with library administration, evaluates and monitors progress pre- and post-survey.
- The Yes! Team, in coordination with library administration, updates training materials.

Consistent Yes-focused Customer Service Standards

- Branch closing announcement: consistent and improved
- Telephone answer script
- Standardized communication when a customer receives a new library card

BRANDING

- Communicate the concept of "yes" customer service to staff, managers, task teams, committees, and all departments—this is a shift in thinking.
- Share Yes! Team training updates at all-staff meetings.
- Create an identity and develop a logo.

OUTPUTS

Evaluate data from an all-staff survey that will identify areas in which staff need/desire more training (technology, customer service, library resources, customers with special needs, safety).

OUTCOMES

- "Yes" staff are happy. When staff are happy, customers are happy.
- Staff who work in an environment of trust are more apt to provide excellent customer service.
- Staff who are knowledgeable in all library products and services can provide personalized service.
- Providing excellent customer service to each other supports each of us individually and collectively.

Yes! Precepts/Miscellaneous

- Be helpful.
- Be solution-oriented.
- Get rid of the professional shield; be real.
- Smile, greet, and learn patrons' names.
- Use jargon-free words (eliminate jargon such as "Claims Returned").
- Teach staff the why and spirit of procedures, not the letter of the law.
- Encourage staff who may resist being empowered to make judgment calls in favor of the customer.
- Shift from service departments dictating to customers what the "rules" are to what the customer wants.
- Say "yes"; it will improve our customers' lives and our own.
- Stop saying "no." We are not cops or wardens.
- Think of ways to meet the customer's needs.
- Change attitude toward people who are unlike ourselves.
- Provide consistency among all branches and CEN.
- Care for our staff by providing decompressing stations for staff to go to after particularly stressful interactions.
- Flip Sierra training around to what we can do, not what we can't do; this is a customer service "yes" approach.
- Keep a "no log" or "obstacles list" at the desk.
- Observe staff interactions while they are working the desk: Why do we say no?

- Identify triggers that initiate "yes" conversations.
- Identify the consequences for staff of not following "yes" protocols.
- Allow patrons to "badge" staff, thus rewarding "yes" customer service.
- When waiving fines to achieve a "yes"-focused outcome, type "yes" in the customer's library account notes field.

Yes! Customer Service Training Development

Sacramento Public Library Strategic Goal 2: Develop and empower staff to create a culture of customer service that ensures positive experiences for our diverse community.

Modular Training

I. What is yes-focused customer service?
    a. Introduction
    b. Strategic plan goals
    c. Key learning objectives

II. The importance of staff
    a. The library's greatest asset
    b. Hold key to customer experience
    c. Connection to library information/resources
    d. Consistent delivery of customer service

III. Acknowledge obstacles to providing yes-focused customer service
    a. Unhappy customers
    b. Abusive customers
    c. Incidents
    d. Managing obstacles
    e. Staff support: permission to acknowledge difficulties; time to decompress
    f. Policy, procedures, rules, "nos!"
        i. Examples of library "nos"
        ii. "No" log

IV. For library administrators, leaders, supervisors
    a. Empower staff to make independent judgment calls without fear
    b. Praise and reward staff
    c. Rate staff on customer experience; tie it to performance

V. Retail models
    a. Why we love our favorite retail store, restaurant, or service
    b. Starbucks, Amazon, Zappos, others

VI. Master the customer transaction—personalize service—BLAST:
    a. Believe
        i. Assume the best

      ii. Make someone's day

      iii. Consistency

      iv. Cultural awareness

  b. Listen

      i. Customer clues

      ii. Observe body language

      iii. Staff toolbox of knowledge

      iv. Staff empathy

      v. Differently-abled customers

  c. Assist

      i. Err on the side of the customer

      ii. Assume the best

      iii. Product or service need

  d. Solve

      i. Overcome "no"

      ii. Own and resolve

      iii. Custom solution

      iv. Judgment call

      v. Personalize service

  e. Thank

      i. Offer personal expression of appreciation

      ii. We want customers to be happy

  f. Other

Things to Keep in Mind

- Make it Fun!
- Use scenarios, role-play, compelling stories, video, and small group discussion.
- Build in time for questions.
- Take time to review.
- Ask for all staff commitment to be yes-focused.
- Gather feedback through training evaluation and surveys.

Selected Bibliography

Albrecht, Steve. *Library Security: Better Communication, Safer Facilities*. Chicago: ALA Editions, 2015.

Bell, Chip R., and John R. Patterson. *Customer Loyalty Guaranteed*. Avon, MA: Adam Business, 2007.

Bliss, Jeanne. *Chief Customer Officer 2.0*. Hoboken, NJ: John Wiley & Sons, 2015.

Branson, Richard. *Like a Virgin*. New York: Penguin, 2012.

Branson, Richard. *The Virgin Way: Everything I Know about Leadership*. New York: Penguin Group, 2014.

Bryant, Adam. *Quick and Nimble*. New York: Henry Holt, 2014.

Buono, Michael. "Risk Looking Stupid." In *Library Services for Multicultural Patrons*, edited by Carol Smallwood and Kim Becnel, 303–308. Lanham, MD: Scarecrow Press, 2013.

Byrne, John A. *World Changers*. New York: Penguin Group, 2011.

Dijulius, John R. *Secret Service: Hidden Systems That Deliver Unforgettable Customer Service*. New York: American Management Association, 2003.

Disney Institute and Theodore B. Kinni. *Be Our Guest*. New York: Disney Editions, 2011.

Ford, Lisa, David McNair, and William Perry. *Exceptional Customer Service*. 2nd ed. Avon, MA: Adams Business, 2009.

Gray, Dave, and Thomas Vander Wal. *The Connected Company*. Sebastopol, CA: O'Reilly, 2012.

Hsieh, Tony. *Delivering Happiness*. New York: Business Plus, 2010.

Hyken, Shep. *The Amazement Revolution*. Austin, TX: Greenleaf, 2011.

Inghilleri, Leonardo, and Micah Solomon. *Exceptional Service, Exceptional Profit*. New York: AMACOM, 2010.

Kaufman, Ron. *Uplifting Service*. New York: Evolve Publishing, 2012.

Leonard, Kelly, and Tom Yorton. *Yes, and: How Improvisation Reverses "No, but" Thinking and Improves Creativity and Collaboration; Lessons from The Second City*. New York: Harbor Business, 2015.

Michelli, Joseph A. *Driven to Delight*. New York: McGraw-Hill Education, 2016.

Michelli, Joseph A. *Leading the Starbucks Way*. New York: McGraw-Hill Education, 2014.

Michelli, Joseph A. *The New Gold Standard: 5 Leadership Principles for Creating a Legendary Customer Experience Courtesy of the Ritz-Carlton Hotel Company.* New York: McGraw-Hill, 2008.

Michelli, Joseph A. *The Starbucks Experience.* New York: McGraw-Hill, 2007.

Shaw, Colin, and John Ivens. *Building Great Customer Experiences.* New York: Palgrave Macmillan, 2002.

Sinek, Simon. *Leaders Eat Last.* New York: Penguin Group, 2014.

Solomon, Micah. *High-Tech, High-Touch Customer Service.* New York: AMACOM, 2012.

Spector, Robert, and Patrick McCarthy. *The Nordstrom Way.* Hoboken, NJ: John Wiley & Sons, 2005.

Stone, Brad. *The Everything Store.* New York: Little, Brown, 2013.

Vaynerchuk, Gary. *The Thank You Economy.* New York: HarperCollins, 2011.

Yellen, Emily. *Your Call Is (Not That) Important to Us.* New York: Free Press, 2009.

Index

About the Author

KATHY L. MIDDLETON, MLIS, is assistant director for public services at Sacramento Public Library (SPL), Sacramento, CA. She joined the SPL team in April 2015, bringing with her nine years of eye-opening public library experiences with people of all ages, backgrounds, and abilities. Collecting customer service stories from library staff and coupling them with her own, she enjoys sharing her thoughts in *Public Libraries Online* and *Public Libraries*. Middleton leads a "Yes! Customer Service Team" at SPL that chronicles and promotes ways in which library service changes lives. A career change led her to return to college, where she completed a bachelor's degree in the history of art at the University of California Berkeley (2002). She also holds a master's degree in museum studies from San Francisco State University (2004) and a master's degree in library and information science from San Jose State University (2006).